VESSELS FOR UNDERWATER EXPLORATION

The research submersible Deep Quest *performs delicate underwater tasks with its twin mechanical arms.*

VESSELS FOR UNDERWATER EXPLORATION

by Peter R. Limburg and James B. Sweeney

CROWN PUBLISHERS, INC., NEW YORK

PHOTOCREDITS

Contents

1

Man Studies the Oceans

IN 1966 a hydrogen bomb was lost in the Mediterranean Sea when a U.S. bomber was destroyed in a midair collision over the coast of Spain. It fell in water nearly half a mile deep. Could the bomb be recovered before the seawater damaged its firing mechanism and triggered a catastrophic explosion?

Ten years earlier the answer would have been no, for the bomb lay far too deep for a diver to reach, and the sea floor was so uneven that a dragnet would not have picked the bomb up. But disaster was averted when the bomb was located and recovered with the aid of two research submersibles, *Alvin* and *Aluminaut*.

What is a submersible, and how is it different from a submarine? A submersible is a vessel designed to operate underwater and also able to float on the surface. A military submarine is a large, fast, armed submersible. But there are also un-

armed submersibles that are used for scientific research, salvage work, and other peaceful underwater tasks. Basically, they are small, highly maneuverable submarines specially equipped for such work.

The first research submersible was launched in 1959. It could carry observers as deep as 1,350 feet. Today there are submersibles that can descend to depths of a mile or more. Such deep-ranging craft have enabled scientists to see, firsthand, things that man had never been able to observe before. They have helped to revolutionize our knowledge of the ocean depths, once as mysterious and inaccessible as outer space.

For thousands of years man has been fascinated by the sea. In its salty waters primitive tribes found fish and shellfish to feast on. Later, fishermen sailed out in their little craft with their nets and lines. As civilization advanced, ships of ancient

The two-man research submersible Alvin *is lowered into the water to begin its search for the missing H-bomb.*

empires traveled over the sea, carrying valuable cargoes of silk and spices and jewels from far-off lands, or daily needs such as grain, timber, and big clay jars filled with wine or olive oil. Over the sea, too, sailed swift ships bearing fierce warriors looking for rich cities to raid or conquer. Near the shore, naked divers searched the shallow waters for pearls and sponges.

Man often feared the sea, with its pounding waves and unpredictable winds and wild storms. Its unmeasurable depths filled him with awe and terror. His imagination peopled the ocean deeps with angry gods and hideous, evil monsters. Nonetheless, this was not enough to frighten man away from the sea.

Over the centuries, men learned how to build better ships and to navigate them more accurately. The sea grew in impor-

tance as a source of food and an avenue of transportation. Yet it was not until the last century that man began to study the seas in a truly scientific way, and not until the middle of this century that he was able to explore deep waters in person.

Oceanography—the study of the ocean—is a very complex science. It includes many other sciences insofar as they have some relationship to the sea. Oceanography includes physics, chemistry, meteorology, geology, and biology. It also uses knowledge from medicine, mathematics, physiology, paleontology, and engineering, plus other specialties too numerous to name here.

Oceanographers may chart the ocean floor, measure the speed and direction of currents, or study the plants and animals that inhabit the various zones of the ocean, from tide flats to the deepest abyss. They study winds and waves and tides, and the temperature and salt content of the water. They study the birth of storms at sea and the paths that they follow. They search the ocean floor for mineral deposits, and they gather information on the breeding and feeding patterns of fish. They monitor the heartbeats of whales, and they study the effects of long, deep dives on human beings. All these things, and many others, are among the specialties of oceanographers.

One of the earliest oceanographic projects was carried out by Benjamin Franklin—a study of the Gulf Stream. In the 1700s, complaints were heard that ships took about two weeks longer to sail from Falmouth, in the southwest of England, to New York than they did from London to Rhode Island, even though the London–Rhode Island route was about two hundred miles longer. More puzzling still, the ships sailing from Falmouth were fast, lightly laden packet ships, the express

Life forms such as this sponge, photographed at a depth of 1,500 feet, were unknown before modern oceanographic techniques were developed.

ships of their day, carrying mail and government dispatches. The ships from London were, for the most part, slow, heavily laden merchant vessels. The English authorities were mystified. They could find no reasons to account for this strange phenomenon. Franklin, who became involved because of his position as postmaster general of the American colonies, had an answer, although the British would not listen.

The answer to the riddle was the Gulf Stream, the vast current of warm water that flows northward along the eastern coast of North America, then swings eastward off Canada and continues across the North Atlantic to Europe. The English packet captains did not know about the Gulf Stream, but the Rhode Islanders who captained the merchant ships did and kept out of its way. New Englanders had learned about the Gulf Stream from sailing the ocean after whales, which often followed the edges of the current though they were seldom found within it. The whalers learned to recognize it by its clear, blue, warm water, so different from the cold, gray water of the North Atlantic that bordered it. This knowledge was passed on to other New England seamen, who made good use of it. British sea captains, however, felt that they were too wise to be counseled by simple American fishermen (as Franklin wrote later) and persisted in trying to sail right up the middle of the Gulf Stream. On the map, this may have been the most direct course to follow. What they did not realize was that, with an unfavorable wind, the current could push them back as much as seventy miles a day.

Franklin began his study of the Gulf

Stream in 1775, but it was interrupted by the American Revolution. In 1785 he began again, this time completing his work.

Few scientific instruments had been invented in Franklin's time, and all he was able to do was to take the temperature of the water and the air above it. This he did at regular intervals, carefully noting down the results. He also took notes on the color of the water and the fish and floating seaweed that he observed in it. From these few clues he was able to make a surprisingly accurate chart of the Gulf Stream's path. How? The water of the Gulf Stream is noticeably warmer than the water of the ocean on either side of it. When the water's temperature changed suddenly, Franklin knew that he had crossed the boundary of the Gulf Stream. He also knew, as he had

learned from New England whalers, that the Gulf Stream had a different color from the surrounding ocean, that few fish swam in it, and that whales were never found in it. He also noted that it contained large quantities of a certain kind of seaweed. He published his findings, and sea captains who cared to follow Franklin's advice were able to cut as much as two weeks off the voyage between Europe and the United States.

Almost a century later, the British naval ship H.M.S. *Challenger* sailed off on a four-year voyage of exploration. The voyage, which lasted from 1872 to 1876 and covered most of the world's oceans, was one of the most important events in the history of oceanography. Information gathered by the *Challenger* turned some of

The four-year voyage of H.M.S. Challenger, *in the 1870s, revolutionized scientists' thinking about the ocean depths.*

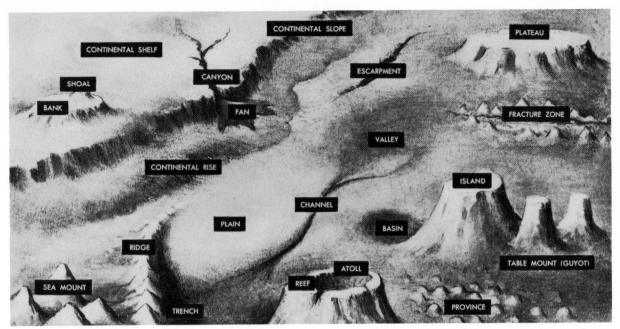

The ocean floor, once thought to be a smooth plain, is actually studded with mountains and canyons, as shown in this drawing.

man's ideas about the deep sea upside down.

By the 1870s, science had provided oceanographers with more instruments, and better ones, than Franklin had. The scientists on the *Challenger* had devices that could take soundings at depths of several miles and bring up samples of the ocean floor. They could collect samples of water at predetermined depths to measure its temperature and analyze its chemical makeup. Deep-running nets, dragged through the water, captured fish and crustaceans that no one had ever seen before. Much valuable information was gathered this way. For example, scientists had previously thought that the ocean floor was a vast plain. The *Challenger*'s soundings showed that it contained rugged mountain peaks and deep chasms, all invisible from the surface. Her nets brought up living creatures from a depth of 14,600 feet, deeper than life had been known to exist.

Still, trying to explore the ocean by taking scattered samples from the surface was a bit like trying to explore the great plains of Africa by flying thousands of feet above

them on a dark night, now and then letting down a grab bucket to see what it brought up. Even such inventions as sonar, which accurately measures the rises and dips in the ocean floor directly beneath the sonar instrument, could give no true picture of what the ocean floor looked like.

The diving suit, invented in the 1830s, permitted a man to go much farther down than the traditional naked divers could manage, and to stay for an hour or more, depending on depth. However, a diver equipped with a suit (often called a suited diver or a helmet diver) is limited by the fact that he is linked to a vessel on the surface by his lifeline and his air hose. He cannot move far from his support vessel. And he cannot stay down indefinitely. The area he can investigate is small.

A helmet diver does not usually venture beyond depths of 100 feet or so. At 100 feet his safe time limit is 120 minutes. As the depth increases, his time limit becomes shorter. At 150 feet, for example, it is 80 minutes. And he must return to the surface very slowly after a deep dive, making frequent decompression stops to avoid the

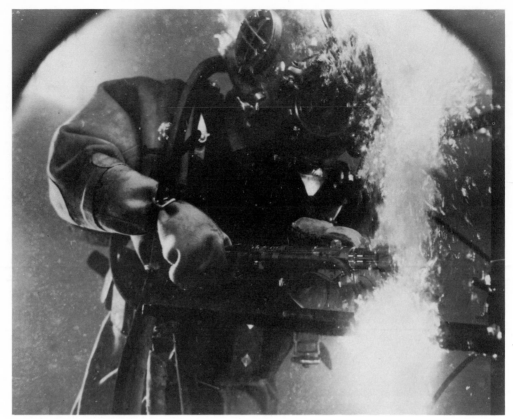

A helmeted diver cuts steel bars with an oxyhydrogen torch, invented for underwater tasks such as salvaging wrecked ships.

"bends," a painful and sometimes fatal condition caused by gas bubbles forming in the diver's bloodstream and joints.

As soon as a diver enters the water, there is pressure against his body. The deeper he goes, the greater the pressure becomes, about 4¼ pounds per square inch for every 10 feet of water. At 33 feet, the pressure on the diver is twice that of the air at the surface. Normal atmospheric pressure is about 14.7 pounds per square inch, or nearly 2,120 pounds per square foot. Thus, only 33 feet down, a diver must carry an extra pressure of *over a ton* on every square foot of his body's surface. This pressure doubles at 66 feet, triples at 99 feet, and so on as the depth increases.

Even three feet below the surface a snorkel tube will not work. The pressure of the water on the diver's chest and back—over two hundred pounds for an average adult—is enough to keep him

from expanding his chest to draw in a breath. To overcome the pressure of the water, the diver must be supplied with air at equal or greater pressure. When the pressure of the air coming through his breathing hose and filling his lungs balances the force of the water pressing against his rib cage, he can breathe normally. But there is danger in this. If the pressure of the air is high enough, nitrogen begins to dissolve in the diver's blood and body fat. (Nitrogen, which makes up about four-fifths of the atmosphere, does not normally dissolve in the body; under high pressure it does.) If the pressure on the diver is reduced rapidly, the nitrogen comes fizzing out of solution like the bubbles in a bottle of soda. The bubbles can block the diver's blood vessels or press against his nerves, causing pain, paralysis, or even death. Therefore the diver must take care to come up slowly, so that the nitrogen can pass out of his system gradually and harmlessly.

A scuba diver is not tied to a surface vessel, as a helmet diver is. He carries his own air supply with him and can move about freely, unencumbered by a heavy, clumsy diving suit. But he must observe the same limits on his time in the water as a helmet diver, and he must go through the same time-consuming decompression process while returning to the surface. A highly trained scuba diver can go down to about three hundred feet for a short period, and brief experimental dives have been made even deeper. But most of the ocean lies far below the reach of the scuba diver.

A scuba-equipped archaeologist plots the position of cargo in an ancient Roman ship that sank over 1,500 years ago.

An underwater scooter delivers oceanographers and their equipment to a coral reef.

The development that has possibly extended man's knowledge of the ocean more than any other is the deep-diving research submersible. These undersea research craft are equipped with viewports, searchlights, and scientific instruments for recording such things as depth and temperature of the water. Some are equipped with mechanical arms, controlled from inside the submersible. The arms can retrieve heavy chunks of rock from the bottom; they can gather delicate living organisms without injuring them. Research submersibles also carry cameras to photograph undersea life-forms and anything else of interest, such as deep-lying wrecks of ships. Such a submersible can gather more information in one dive than a scuba diver can get in weeks of work.

The oceanographic submersible has other advantages. Because its hull is rigid, it does not need to be filled with high-pressure air to resist the pressure of the water surrounding it. The crew inside can work comfortably at normal atmospheric pressure. They can remain submerged for as long as their air and power supply hold out. Oceanographic submersibles can also be made to withstand pressures far greater than those an ordinary submarine can take. One submersible, the *Trieste,* descended 35,800 feet to the floor of the deepest trench in the Pacific Ocean. This was nearly seven miles, and the pressure on the *Trieste* was over seven tons per square inch!

Related to the submersible is the undersea habitat, a large chamber filled with a special "breathing mixture" of oxygen and helium. The habitat serves as a base of operations for scuba divers. Unlike ordinary scuba divers, these men and women live in the habitat between dives. The pressure in the habitat is the same as that

Scuba divers monitor operations of Star III.

of the water outside, so there is no danger of the bends. The divers can spend long periods of time beneath the sea, uninterrupted by the need to return to the surface. In an experiment conducted by the United States Navy, teams of divers spent up to 15 days beneath the surface at a depth of 205 feet, making occasional dives below the 300-foot mark. In a separate experiment conducted by Jacques-Yves Cousteau, 6 oceanauts spent a month living and working at a depth of 328 feet. Plans have already been made for habitats in which men and women will live at depths of 800 feet or more for weeks at a time, exploring the ocean and all that it contains.

This book will trace the high points of the story of man's exploration of the sea, from the men who dived for sponges and pearls in early times to modern oceanographic submersibles and undersea habitats. It will include the development of diving suits, diving bells, and scuba gear, since these are part of the history of man's penetration of the depths.

From the very beginning, most of the world's undersea craft were intended for use as warships, and most of the improvements in their design were invented in response to the needs of war. It was in military submarines that man first navigated beneath the surface of the water, and it was this success that gave him the confidence to venture deeper. To write this book without including the history of military submarines would mean beginning in the late 1950s. Only then did governments, which have the money to carry on such projects, become seriously interested in developing research submersibles. And this, in turn, was because the newly developed

nuclear submarines—military craft—needed more accurate information about the deep-sea floor and the currents that sweep over it, information that could not be obtained by divers nor by observations from surface ships. At this point, our focus shifts to the peaceful exploration of the depths, where new frontiers are constantly being opened to man.

The ocean depths are in some ways much like outer space. Both, until recently, were filled with unimaginable mysteries. Both were impossible to reach until technology gave man the means of getting there. Both are hostile environments; that is, man cannot survive in either one without elaborate life-support systems. The men who are most familiar with the depths often call them "inner space." In some ways, inner space is more difficult to explore than outer space. Yet the sea is close at hand, as the stars and the planets are not.

2

The Dawn of Underwater Exploration

WHEN did man first begin to explore the world beneath the sea? Nobody knows exactly, but perhaps his first step was gathering shellfish from rocks and mud flats at low tide thousands of years ago. We know that primitive man ate shellfish, because he left huge heaps of discarded shells after he had eaten the animal inside. Some of these shell heaps may be as much as thirty-five thousand years old.

From gathering shellfish at low water it is not a big step to wading in water up to your waist, or even deeper, and sticking your head down for a quick look—or even learning how to swim beneath the surface for a few brief moments. Although we cannot be certain, this is probably how primitive man lost some of his fear of the water. In any case, some venturesome individuals did sooner or later learn how to dive beneath the surface. By 2500 B.C. the Chinese were gathering pearls and pearl

shell from the sea. Since the pearl oyster does not grow near the surface, this had to be done by diving. The ancient Greeks were gathering sponges and oysters from the coastal waters of the Mediterranean Sea as long ago as 1000 B.C., and they may simply have been following the example of civilizations that came before them.

These men worked naked, as did all divers before the invention of diving gear many centuries later, and they had no breathing devices. Their only equipment was a knife for prying loose sponges or oysters, and sometimes a net bag for carrying their booty to the surface. Sometimes the diver would coat his skin with oil or grease to give him some protection against the chill of the water. Often he clutched a heavy stone to help him descend to the bottom quickly. This saved seconds of precious time—even an experienced diver can rarely hold his breath for much more than

This old engraving shows pearl divers in the Indian Ocean. At upper left, a diver descends with the aid of a heavy stone.

two minutes, and his breath has to last him from the time he enters the water until he reaches the surface again. The faster he reaches the bottom, the more time he has for the work he went down to do.

The little kingdoms and republics of ancient Greece were usually not on friendly terms with each other. They engaged in many bitter struggles for supremacy. Much of the action in these wars took place at sea, and Greek divers played an important part in some of the battles. They cut the anchor ropes of enemy ships, leaving them to drift to destruction on rocks and reefs. They tore down defensive barricades of stakes in the water. Swimming under water, safely out of sight of their attackers, they towed leather bags filled with provisions to besieged garrisons.

Greek divers may have used some kind of breathing tube, like a modern snorkel, for underwater dives close to the surface. The famous philosopher Aristotle (384–322 B.C.) made a tantalizing reference to a breathing device in one of his writings, but he neglected to describe it, other than to compare it to an elephant's trunk. Perhaps he thought that such a breathing device would be well known to any of his readers. Or he may simply have felt that it didn't have much to do with the main subject of his discussion, which was elephants.

Aristotle was the tutor of Alexander the Great (356–323 B.C.), one of the greatest military leaders of the ancient world. Alexander acquired a lively curiosity about science from Aristotle, and there is a legend that he had himself lowered into the sea in a glass barrel to observe for himself the fabled monsters of the undersea world. According to one version of the legend, Alexander took along two secre-

A 16th-century artist of India painted this fanciful picture of Alexander the Great's legendary visit to the depths.

taries to take notes on what he observed.

It is hard to tell whether there is any truth to this legend, but perhaps Alexander really did make a brief submergence in some sort of diving bell with glass viewports. During his time, Greek sponge divers were using a primitive type of diving bell to enable them to stay underwater longer to collect more sponges. Aristotle described it as a large, inverted kettle, filled with air, which was lowered through the water to the level where the divers were working. The divers could then swim to the kettle when they needed a new lungful of air.

This air kettle was an early step along the road to undersea exploration, for a good air supply allows a diver to stay underwater long enough to make observations.

Julius Caesar (102?–44 B.C.), the famous Roman general, used divers in his military campaigns, and diving seems to have become a standard feature of naval tactics by late Roman times. Roman naval divers performed the same sorts of missions as modern frogmen, except that they could not plant explosive charges, since explosives had not yet been invented.

The Romans also used divers in attempts to recover valuable cargoes from ships that had sunk in fairly shallow water. (The limit for most divers, in those days before the invention of the diving suit or scuba gear, was about thirty feet, as it still is for a diver without such equipment.)

When the Roman Empire broke up in A.D. 476, after a long period of decay, diving became almost a lost skill—at least in Europe. Here and there, medieval chroniclers recount the use of divers in warfare. For example, in A.D. 1000 a Viking pirate named Oddo attacked another group of Vikings. Under cover of darkness, the defenders sent divers under Oddo's ships to bore holes through their stout oak planking. Oddo's men, working frantically to keep their ships from sinking, could not fight off the defending warriors, and all of them lost their lives.

During the Crusades a diver carried messages to and from the Arab seaport city of Acre, which was besieged by the crusaders. And in 1203, divers reportedly destroyed an underwater stockade protecting a fortified island in the Seine River, in

France. But exploits such as these were very rare, and they were always reported as something very much out of the ordinary.

Some medieval scholars, however, fantasized about devices that would enable men to spend an extended period of time underwater—hours, perhaps, or even days. One such imaginative scholar was Roger Bacon, a brilliant English monk of the thirteenth century, who also predicted that men would someday travel through the air.

Bacon wrote a good deal about the possi-

A diver breathes air from a gourd in this 16th-century illustration.

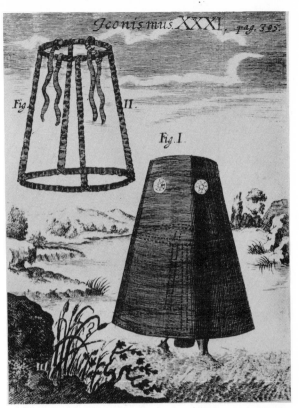

This portable diving bell of the 1600s was designed to be made of leather and metal.

bility of divers using air hoses for breathing, but he gave no details for his scheme. He also claimed that such air hoses had been made in ancient times and were also being made in his own day; however, he did not give any proof of this claim. Perhaps, as was the case with most of his writings, Bacon was being purposely vague in order to stay out of trouble with his superiors in the Catholic Church.

Bacon's proposal for a diver's breathing apparatus never went beyond the paper it was written on. This was the usual fate of most ideas for technical inventions until modern times. Inventors lacked the proper materials and tools for turning their ideas into reality. And most of them were without any knowledge of scientific principles, so that the inventions they planned would not have worked even if they could have been built. Hundreds of years of experiments would have to be made, with men learning from their failures, before science and technology reached the point where a workable breathing apparatus for a diver could be made.

The earliest known design for a diving helmet appeared in 1511. It consisted of a waterproof leather hood that enclosed the diver's head and tapered up to a slender hose, also of leather, at its top. The other end of the hose was buoyed up by a float on the surface. This helmet had a serious

Leonardo da Vinci designed this spiked helmet for a military diver. It would not have stood the test of use.

Model of an impractical diving suit. The diver, blinded by his hood, could not have breathed due to water pressure on his chest.

flaw: the diver would have had to work blind, because no viewports were provided for him to see out of. In any case, it would not have worked because its designer did not realize that an air pump was needed to keep the diver breathing, on account of the pressure of the water.

About the same time, Leonardo da Vinci designed an armored diving suit for a military diver. Although Leonardo is best known today as a great artist, he was also a great engineer, inventor, and military strategist. Leonardo's design was realistic enough to include a glass faceplate for the diver, allowing him to see his work. The diving outfit would be classed as a scuba rig, since the air supply was contained in a leather wine sack. The water would press on the sack just as hard as it did on the diver's chest, so that the diver would be able to breathe comfortably, at least in theory. The design might have worked, had such a diving suit ever been made, but the leather sack would not have contained enough air for anything but a short dive.

A more practical idea of Leonardo's was swim fins for hands and feet.

Leonardo's design also provided the diver with some small, empty leather bags to inflate when he had completed his job; these were then to float him quickly to the surface. Unfortunately, Leonardo overlooked the fact that inflating the bags would require extra air, which the diver had no way of getting.

Another ingenious but impractical design was published in 1551 by a famous Italian mathematician named Niccolò Tartaglia. Tartaglia's design looked something like an hourglass with the bottom half missing. At the top of a tall, wooden frame was mounted a large glass bowl, open at the bottom, which was to cover the diver's head and hold a supply of air. The diver himself stood on a platform at the bottom of the framework. To operate the apparatus, the diver dropped a heavy weight overboard, then cranked himself down to the bottom by means of a windlass and a rope attached to the weight. Once at the bottom, the diver could presumably make short trips out into the water, returning to his glass bowl to breathe.

One weak point in the design was that subsurface pressure would have forced water up into the glass bowl, compressing the air into a small space at the top of the bowl and making it difficult for the diver to reach. At a depth of thirty-three feet, for example, the air would be compressed into half the space it had occupied at the surface.

Some practical progress was also being made in the 1500s. An Italian diver, using a diving rig of his own invention, was able

This model of Tartaglia's diving "hourglass" shows how a diver was supposed to crank himself down to the bottom.

to stay submerged for more than an hour, moving about freely on the bottom. (He was attempting to salvage an ancient Roman ship sunk in Lake Nemi.) This diving outfit was essentially a small diving bell that the diver carried around with him. The bell covered only the upper half of the diver, leaving his hands free to perform work; a viewport gave him a limited amount of visibility. The bell was supported partly by straps resting on the diver's shoulders and partly by a rope attached to a support at the surface. Presumably the diver did not go deep enough for the water pressure to squeeze the air into an inconveniently small space. Also, because the bell covered not only his head but his chest as well, it gave him a larger air supply to begin with than Tartaglia's design provided.

Occasionally, entertainers put on diving exhibitions. Their stunts were simple, but diving was so little known that to most people they appeared nothing short of miraculous.

One such exhibition took place in 1538 at Toledo, an ancient Spanish city perched on a crag overlooking the swift Tagus River. Two Greeks descended into the river in a diving bell described as "a very large kettle," taking with them a lighted candle! When they were pulled up, not only were both men completely dry, but their candle was still burning! This exhibition took place before an audience of nearly ten thousand spectators, including the Emperor Charles V. It was fortunate that the emperor was there, for otherwise no one might have bothered to record the happening. In those days, it took the presence of an important person to make an event worth writing about.

Around the same time, the use of divers in warfare was apparently increasing, for the list of equipment on one English warship included ten "kettlehats" for divers. These were presumably helmets designed to protect the divers against bullets and arrows shot at them from the surface. They may have been forerunners of the modern rigid diving helmet, which protects the diver's head while it permits him to breathe.

A picture of a diver recovering cannon from the water appeared in a Spanish book on artillery in the mid-1500s. The diver, who is busy attaching a sling to a large cannon barrel, is equipped with a leather hood attached to a jacket covering his upper body and his arms down to the wrists. A leather breathing tube extends

In this 16th-century Spanish diagram, a diver attaches hoisting slings to a cannon barrel.

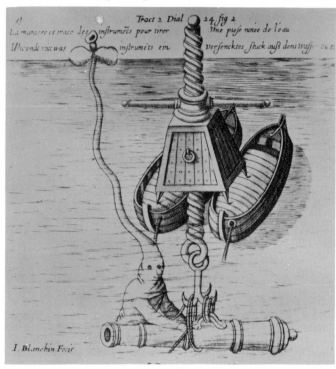

from the top of the hood to the surface, where its free end is held clear of the water by a float.

Had an air pump been provided, this outfit might actually have worked. However, as explained earlier, the diver could not have breathed with the equipment pictured. Impractical as this design was, however, it shows that men were once more thinking about doing work underwater.

A noted English scientist, Sir Francis Bacon (no relation to Roger Bacon), left a description of a diving bell among his writings. From the way in which Bacon described the device, it would seem to have been in actual use. This diving bell stood well clear of the bottom, supported on three legs, so that the diver could easily leave it and return for a new breath.

New designs for diving bells began to appear more frequently toward the close of the 1500s. Some of the most advanced came from Venice, which was then one of Europe's leading cities in matters of technology and maritime engineering.

The late 1500s also saw the world's first detailed description of a submarine. Published in 1578 by an Englishman named William Bourne, it was a source of ideas for other would-be submarine inventors for many years. Although Bourne left no drawings or models, and never built an actual submarine, his writing was clear enough to give a good idea of what he had in mind.

The boat was to have an airtight, two-decked hull, fitted with air pockets for buoyancy. Air for breathing was to come through a hollow mast extending above the surface. In order to make the boat submerge, Bourne proposed to decrease its

buoyancy by means of very large, movable plungers that worked inside cylinders whose outer ends were open to the water. The plungers were to be operated by giant screws, like those used on printing presses in Bourne's time. When the plungers were screwed inward, water would enter the cylinders, increasing the boat's weight until it sank. When they were screwed outward, the water was forced out, making the boat that much lighter. Somewhat the same principle is used in modern submarines, except that they let water into ballast tanks through valves and blow it out by means of high-pressure air.

Thus, by the end of the 1500s, the idea of divers working underwater for long periods of time was no longer considered outlandish, at least not by scientists and engineers of the time. Some practical progress had been made in the design and use of diving bells, and a well-thought-out plan for a submersible craft had been published. Tools and materials for the construction of simple diving equipment were now available, as were workmen with the skill to make the equipment, and military and salvage divers with the daring to wear it.

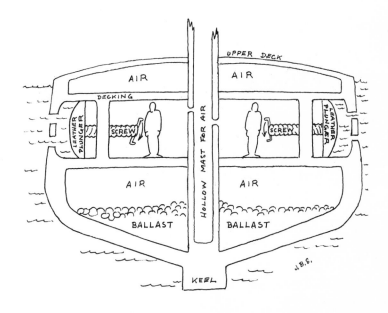

A simple diagram of William Bourne's design for a submarine boat, based on Bourne's own description.

3

Pioneers of Underwater Boats and Bells

THE theories worked out in the late 1500s, combined with the practical achievements of salvage divers, led to some remarkable progress in the development of underwater craft. As early as the 1620s (the exact date is not known), a functioning submersible vessel was constructed by Cornelis Drebbel, a Dutchman who had followed the trail of fortune to England.

Drebbel, born in the Dutch town of Alkmaar in 1573, was a man of many talents: artist, mathematician, chemist, physicist, and engineer. He had come to England about 1604, and his scientific experiments had so fascinated King James I that the scholarly monarch had given him a royal subsidy to continue them. One of Drebbel's inventions was a "perpetual motion" machine that became one of the wonders of its day; another was a glass globe within which he could supposedly produce rain, hail, thunder, lightning, and

frost at any time. Among his more practical achievements were a method of dyeing wool and silk a brilliant scarlet (a method which gave a great boost to the English textile industry), and a self-regulating furnace that would hold the temperature steady at the degree of heat for which it was set, one of the earliest examples of a feedback mechanism. He was also involved in the great project of draining vast swamplands in eastern England to turn them into farmland, and he was in charge of the fire ships on a naval expedition against France. (A fire ship was an unmanned ship packed to the gunwales with gunpowder, tar, and other highly inflammable substances. In battle, it was set afire and allowed to drift toward the enemy's ships, hopefully colliding and setting them on fire or blowing them up.) Drebbel may also have been the first scientist in England to use the microscope, telescope, and thermometer. The fact that a first-rate thinker like Drebbel was involved in submarine inventions is evidence that underwater ships were now being taken quite seriously.

Unfortunately, no reliable description of Drebbel's boat has come down to us, but a number of people have mentioned it in diaries and books. According to these reports, it was propelled by twelve oarsmen and could submerge to a depth of about fifteen feet. Like all ships at that time, it was built of wood. It was covered with heavily greased leather to make it watertight. Leather seals kept the entrance hatch from leaking. Apparently the boat had glass viewports, since one chronicler reported that its passengers could see well enough underwater to read the Bible without the aid of candlelight.

Its most interesting feature was a system for keeping the air inside the submersible fit for breathing while it was beneath the surface. With his scientific training, Drebbel somehow guessed that only a part of the air was used in breathing, and, without

knowing about oxygen (which was not discovered until a century and a half later), he invented a system for regenerating the atmosphere in his submersible. From another English scientist's notes, we know that he used some kind of chemical solution, either to supply fresh oxygen or to soak up excess carbon dioxide, but Drebbel kept his formula a secret, and it was lost.

Drebbel's submarine made a number of trips up and down the Thames River in the neighborhood of London; supposedly it could travel five miles in each direction without coming up for air. (In one direction, the current may have helped the oarsmen, who must have encountered increased resistance underwater.)

King James himself made at least one trip underwater, and some historians believe that the king was so impressed by his underwater excursion that he ordered the building of two submarines for military use, plus a supply of underwater mines. It is thought that Drebbel was in charge of

An artist's conception of Drebbel's oar-powered submersible of the early 1620s. This drawing does not show viewports.

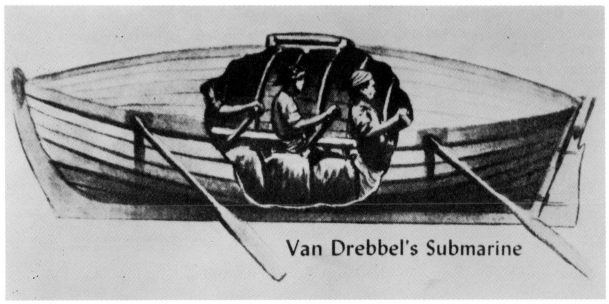

Van Drebbel's Submarine

this project, which apparently continued secretly after his death in 1634. No practical results, however, are known.

Drebbel was not the only prominent man of science connected with submersible development. In 1634 a French scholar-priest, Father Marin Mersenne, together with a naval chaplain named Georges Fournier, wrote a book on submersible design. Mersenne was a noted mathematician and physicist, who exchanged ideas with leading scientists all over Europe. Fournier, a former professor of mathematics, was also a geographer, author of books on navigation, and collector of facts and folklore about the sea.

Although the two priests never built an actual boat, their ideas were so practical that some are still used in submersible design today. They were the first to propose that an underwater ship be made of metal, which is both stronger than wood and easier to make watertight. They also proposed that it should have a cylindrical shape tapering to a point at each end. This shape, they pointed out, would let the boat pass through the water with little resistance. As an added advantage, the double-ended design would permit the boat to reverse its direction without the need for turning around, a handy feature in a tight situation. Modern submersibles use some other ideas first proposed by Fathers Mersenne and Fournier: air pumps, an escape hatch, and a visual system for seeing above water when the vessel is submerged. They also suggested wheels to allow the boat to run along the bottom, a feature which has not been found practical for modern submersibles, since we now know that the ocean bottom is often too

rough and uneven, or so soft that a wheeled vehicle would sink in and become helplessly mired. Like Drebbel's boat, this craft was also to be propelled by oars, the most reliable method of ship propulsion until the invention of the steam engine.

The submersible designed by the two priests was not intended for peaceful exploration of the seas, however, for it was armed with a heavy-caliber cannon. Early designers were preoccupied with the military uses of submersible craft and neglected their peaceful potential. In fact, down to the late 1800s almost every submersible built or even planned was intended for military purposes.

One of the few exceptions was a submarine constructed in France about 1640 for use in salvage work. Built by order of the king, this boat apparently performed successfully—so successfully, in fact, that a great deal was written about the valuable goods it recovered from the bottom of the sea, but nothing was written about the submarine itself.

The next submersible known to be attempted was a military vessel constructed in the Netherlands in 1653. England and the Netherlands at that time were competing bitterly for supremacy in the highly profitable fishing and merchant shipping trades, and in 1653 they were fighting one of several small, vicious naval wars. The builder of the boat, a Frenchman named De Son, announced that his submarine would "kill the English under water." Wealthy Dutchmen, combining patriotism with the chance to destroy their business rivals, supplied the money for the wonder boat's construction.

De Son made ambitious claims for his

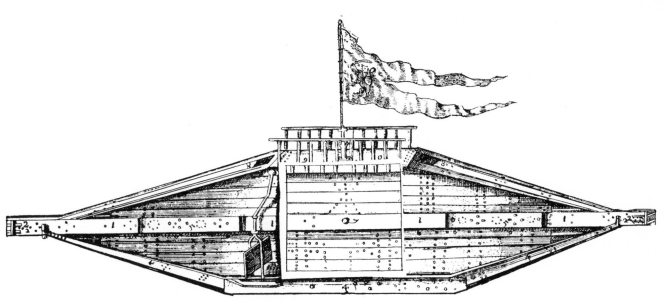

De Son's submarine of 1653. The paddlewheel is concealed in the square box amidships.

submarine: it could travel with the speed of a bird; it could go from Rotterdam (the Netherlands port where it was built) to London and back in a single day, and to the East Indies in six weeks (sailing ships of that day required months for such a trip). Furthermore, it could sink 100 ships a day, even pursuing them into protected harbors; immune to fire, storms, and bullets, it could be captured only by treachery.

In designing his submarine, De Son was very much influenced by the writings of an English churchman interested in mathematics and philosophy, Bishop John Wilkins, who in turn drew upon ideas developed earlier by Drebbel, Fournier, and Mersenne. Bigger than any submersible attempted before, De Son's boat measured seventy-two feet long, eight feet wide, and twelve feet high. An old illustration shows the double-ended shape with the pointed ends that Mersenne and Fournier had ad-

vocated. The ends of the wooden submersible were reinforced with stout iron bars for ramming enemy ships beneath the waterline. It was to be driven by a concealed paddle wheel located amidships and powered by clockwork.

The clockwork machinery that was to supply power worked satisfactorily while the submarine was on the ways of the shipyard. One winding provided power for eight hours as the paddle wheel groaned around and around in the damp Dutch air. Unfortunately for De Son, when the boat was launched, the paddle wheel wouldn't turn at all. The springs and gear wheels of the clockwork mechanism, which had worked so beautifully on dry land, were not strong enough to move the paddles against the resistance of the water. De Son had ignored this factor in his calculations. Unable to get his deadly weapon anywhere under its own power, the disgraced inventor moored it at a wharf and exhibited it as a curiosity, charging a small admission fee to visitors.

De Son failed because he did not choose to face an inconvenient but obvious fact—any boatman could have told him that it was much harder to move an oar through the water than through the air. But the lack of scientific knowledge was a more serious problem than lack of common sense. Even leading scientists of that day knew very little about the way water resists objects moving through it, or the way pressure increases beneath the surface. They knew even less about what increased pressure could do to wood, metal, or human bodies. Experimental science was still in its infancy. Lacking the basic facts they needed, submersible designers had to proceed on guesswork. Most of the time they guessed wrong.

While various plans for military submarines were being developed and found lacking, considerable progress was made in the use of diving bells for salvage. One notable success was the use of a diving bell in 1665 to recover cannons from a Spanish warship—one of the Spanish Armada—that had been wrecked off the coast of Scotland nearly eighty years before. Historians of science have never agreed who deserves the credit for designing this diving bell—a Scottish philosophy professor named George Sinclair or a German scholar named Sturmius—but the important thing is that it *was* built and used successfully.

At about the same time, Spanish divers were using a large bell to recover gold coins from a treasure ship that had gone down at Cadaqués, on the northeast coast of Spain. This bell, made of wood rein-

A model of the 16th-century Scottish diving bell. The bell's wall is cut away to show the diver's position.

forced by iron hoops, measured thirteen or fourteen feet in height and about nine feet across the bottom. Heavy metal balls, weighing sixty to eighty pounds apiece, hung from the lip of the bell to weight it down.

The bell was suspended by a cable and pulley from a sturdy wooden beam supported between two boats. Straining crewmen lowered and raised it by means of a hand-powered winch. The diver, seated on a crossbar in the middle of the bell, com-

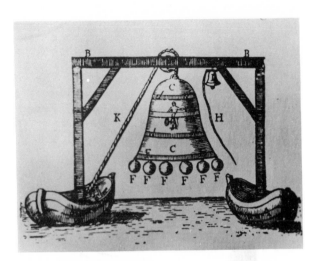

The diving bell used to recover gold coins at Cadaqués, Spain. Artist has drawn in diver to show his position.

municated with the surface crew by means of a rope that led to a small signal bell on the framework of the hoist. When the bell had reached the depth of the wreck, the diver rang the signal bell, and the crew stopped the winch. He then swam out beneath the lip of the bell, which was held some distance off the bottom, and scooped coins into a small sack hung around his neck. When the sack was full—or when he ran out of breath, whichever happened first—he swam back to the bell and emptied it into other sacks suspended from the framework of the bell. After catching his breath, he swam back out again, shuttling back and forth between the bell and the wreck until the air inside the bell became uncomfortably hot and stuffy. This was his warning to signal the surface crew to hoist the bell back topside. The diver's pay consisted of as many coins as he could carry in both hands and his mouth.

Cannons from sunken warships, not treasure, were the main objects of salvage divers' work. The sophisticated equipment needed for discovering lost treasure from wrecks whose location was not known was hundreds of years in the future—but cannons could be spotted fairly easily. Cannons could also stand rough handling while being winched up to the surface, while a treasure chest might burst open, spilling its contents on the ocean floor beyond hope of recovery.

In addition, cannons were worth a great deal of money, not only as weapons but for the metal they contained. In the 1600s, metals cost a great deal to produce; as a result, they were scarce and expensive. Whenever possible, people saved worn-out metal articles to be melted down and used over again. If a cannon was not too badly corroded by the seawater, it could be cleaned out and used again; otherwise, it was good for a ton or two of valuable bronze or iron. Naturally, naval commanders lost no chance of recovering such valuable equipment.

Spurred by this demand, salvage diving in turn spurred the development of better diving equipment, and knowledge gained from diving-bell operations was later put to use by submersible inventors.

About 1690 an English scientist named Edmund Halley designed a diving bell with a continuous air supply. Best known as an astronomer—he discovered the orbit of Halley's comet—Halley was also a pioneer oceanographer and a skilled engineer. He studied the work of earlier inventors, selecting those ideas that had worked best in practice. He combined these ideas with the latest scientific discoveries to produce the most effective diving bell designed up to then.

Halley's diving bell was a milestone in the development of underwater equipment, for its continuous supply of fresh air enabled divers to work for several hours at a stretch. The crews of earlier diving bells had to rely on the air contained in the bell when it was sent down, which was usually used up in less than an hour. In a sense, Halley's bell was the ancestor of today's undersea habitats.

Halley took great care in the design and construction of the bell, which was shaped like a large cone with the pointed end cut off. It measured three feet across the top, five feet across the bottom, and about five feet in height, and it could hold several divers seated comfortably on a bench about a foot above the lower edge. A platform on which the divers could stand hung three feet below the lip of the bell. The bell was built of wood, heavily tarred to preserve it and make it water-repellent. It was sheathed in a thick skin of sheet lead that weighed over half a ton: the lead sheathing made the bell watertight and also supplied part of the weight needed to make the bell sink in the water. Otherwise, the air trapped inside would have kept it afloat like a gigantic upside-down bucket. The rest of the needed weight—over three-and-a-half tons in all—was supplied by loose weights hung from iron rings near the bottom of the bell. This arrangement provided stability and kept the bell from being tipped over by unexpected undersea currents (which would have been very dangerous for the divers).

In the top of the bell was a glass view-

Divers in this 18th-century print are using an improved form of Halley's bell. Note air cask (inaccurately drawn) at right.

port to admit light—another "first" for Halley—and a valve to let stale air out. The sides also had viewports so that the divers could see where they were. This often must have saved valuable time in locating the wreck so that they could begin immediately, without swimming off in the wrong direction. The viewports would also have been valuable for making scientific observations of undersea life. But no scientist of that day—including Halley—was interested.

Of all the features of this diving bell, the air-supply system was Halley's greatest contribution. Lead-covered barrels, filled with air at the surface, were let down to the bell on ropes. Each barrel had a hole in the bottom through which water could enter and compress the air, and a leather

hose coming out of the top to let the air out. The free end of the hose was weighted so that it hung down below the barrel. This kept the air from escaping while the barrel was being lowered, because the pressure of the water at the mouth of the hose was always a little greater than the pressure around the barrel. In a sense, it was like using the water pressure as a cork.

The barrel was lowered a few feet below the bell, and a waiting diver seized the hose and brought it up inside the bell. As soon as the end of the hose was raised above the level of the barrel, the water pressure forced the air through the hose into the bell. (Because of the slight additional depth, the pressure of the water on the barrel was greater than that of the air inside the bell.)

Halley's principle was used in the 19th century. These two variations of the Halley bell were taken from a French book.

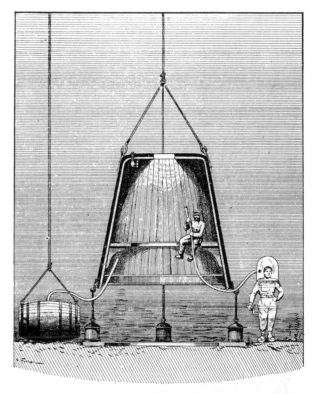

Halley tested the bell himself, going down with four other men to a depth of ten fathoms (sixty feet), where they remained for an hour and a half. As the bell was lowered, the increased water pressure began to squeeze the air into a smaller space, and water began to rise in the bell. Halley therefore stopped every twelve feet and let more air in from his barrels to keep the water down. He found that he needed three to four barrels of air at each stop to keep himself and his companions dry. By keeping the bell filled with compressed air Halley was able to reach depths greater than any diving bell had been able to reach before. A bell without this feature would have been three-quarters filled with water at sixty feet, and divers would have had a hard time reaching the air space.

Some historians have wondered why Halley chose to use barrels for his air supply, rather than bellows or an air pump at the surface. Bellows had been in use for thousands of years, and blacksmiths often had very large ones. It would not have been hard to construct a bellows large enough to supply air to a diving bell, although the leather of the bellows' flexible sides might not have been able to withstand the pressure necessary to force air down to sixty feet below the surface.

Air pumps, a fairly new invention in Halley's day, were also well known. In fact, a French scientist named Denis Papin had proposed using a bellows or a pump to supply air to diving bells a few years earlier. (Papin's idea for using a pump to supply air to diving bells developed from an entirely different project. As an aid to the fishing industry, Papin hoped to use a pump to supply air to a candle burning under a bell whose light would attract schools of fish.) Perhaps Halley feared that a pump might break down just when it was needed most, for pumps were made of metal, and metal objects in those days often contained hidden flaws which made them break under a heavy load.

Halley made a further contribution to underwater exploration by inventing a diving suit to be used with his bell. This was an airtight leather coverall with a glass viewplate in the helmet. Air came via a hose leading into the air space inside the diving bell. This permitted the diver to move about with a good deal of freedom in the neighborhood of the bell without having to come back every few minutes to gulp a breath of air. Halley designed several versions of this diving suit, improving it each time. One version had an all-glass helmet that greatly increased the diver's vision.

Halley's diving bell was a milestone. It proved that divers could be supplied with air many feet below the surface and could work for long periods. It also extended the range of underwater operations to depths that would have been impossible to reach before. In years to come, other men would progress far beyond Halley's achievements, but it was largely Halley's work that made it possible.

4

Daring Inventors

MOMENTUM was gathering in the 1700s. Several Englishmen invented submersibles, using theories worked out by men a century or more earlier. One made a daring dive to win a bet, but never returned to claim his winnings. Another Englishman invented a maneuverable diving chamber, which he used for a highly successful salvage business. Toward the end of the century, during the American Revolution, the submersible had its first trial in actual warfare.

In 1578, when Shakespeare was a teen-aged country boy, William Bourne had published plans for a submarine. A century and a half later, in Devonshire, in the southwest of England, a carpenter named Nathaniel Symons built a submersible using Bourne's principle for regulating the boat's buoyancy. His boat, built around 1729, had a hull made in two sections. They were joined in the middle by a flex-ible leather sheath that could expand and contract like a bellows. By means of a screw arrangement, Symons could tele-scope the hull in and out. The more the hull was expanded, the lighter it became in relation to the water it displaced. The more it was telescoped in, the heavier it became in relation to the water, causing it to sink. Heavy lead weights beneath the keel acted as sinkers and kept the boat in an upright position. Symons added an ad-vanced feature to his "diving boat," a double door through which he could leave and reenter the boat underwater. There is no record that he used it, however.

According to the inventor, this amateur-built submersible descended to the bottom of the Dart River and remained there for three-quarters of an hour. Apparently he had no means of propelling it, however, so that all he could do was submerge and rise again. This in itself was no small triumph, however, considering how many other submersible inventors never came back up.

Well before 1700 a gifted Italian priest-biologist named Borelli had designed a number of devices for undersea exploration, including diving bells, scuba gear, and an underwater boat. The boat, according to Borelli's diagram, was to be propelled by oars and carry an air supply in inflated goatskins. Since ancient times, animal skins had been a common type of container for water and wine. They are also fairly airtight, a quality that Borelli planned to utilize. The skins were to be inflated with air, which would be squeezed out of them with a lever as it was needed. The idea was not altogether impractical. If the boat had ever been built, the skins might have provided enough air for an hour or so. The oars would not have worked well, however, because of the resistance of the water against them on the recovery stroke.

Borelli died in 1679—the book containing his plans came out shortly afterward—but his ideas did not die. An Englishman came across them and used them in building a submersible around 1747. However, instead of using the goatskins as air reservoirs, he used them as buoyancy chambers. In the bottom of the submersible were a series of openings. Each one had a leather sack fastened tightly over it. The necks of the sacks were tied off with cords to keep water from entering. When the sacks were opened, water rushed into them, adding to the weight of the boat and making it sink. To halt the sinking, or to make the boat rise, the water was squeezed out of the sacks. The boat was supposed to be propelled by oars with ingenious folding blades. Designed on the principle of a duck's webbed foot, these blades were supposed to fold up on the recovery stroke, reducing the resistance of the water, and open out like a fan on the power stroke. This system would still not have worked well, however, due to the drag on the oar shafts.

This boat was not a true submersible.

This design for a "diving boat" was based on Borelli's ideas. The man is forcing water out of leather bags to increase buoyancy.

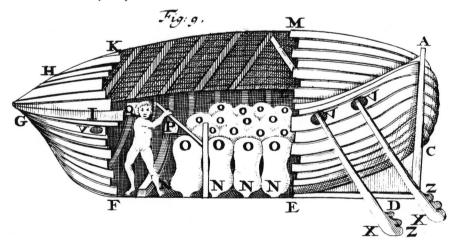

When the sacks were completely filled with water, it floated just awash (that is, even with the surface of the water). But its buoyancy regulation, crude as it was, worked on the same principle as that of modern submarines. The difference is that modern submarines use steel tanks instead of leather bags, and they get rid of the water ballast by blowing it out with compressed air instead of forcing it out by hand.

The year 1715 saw the development of an ingenious one-man diving chamber by a Devonshire farmer named John Lethbridge. (Devonshire men were prominent in this stage of submersible history, perhaps because Devonshire had always been closely involved with the sea. In fact, Devonshire has produced far more than its share of outstanding English seamen.) Unlike most of the inventors before him, Lethbridge sensibly conducted a series of experiments before entrusting his life to his invention. As he told the story in a magazine article many years later:

My thoughts turned to a machine to recover wrecks lost in the sea. The first step I took towards it was going into a hogshead [a large barrel] on land, bung'd up tight, where I stayed half an hour without communication of air. Then I made a trench near a well at the bottom of my orchard, in order to obtain a sufficient quantity of water to cover the hogshead, and then tried to find how long I could live under water, without air-pipes or communication with the air, and found I could stay longer under water than upon land.

Lethbridge could not have been very

A model of John Lethbridge's diving cask, constructed according to his own description.

comfortable hunched up in his barrel, but he was now sure that he could survive for some time in a tightly closed container. The next step was to have a working model of his salvage device built.

Wisely preferring not to take unnecessary chances, Lethbridge had the diving chamber built to his specifications by a cooper, or professional barrelmaker. Made of sturdy planks, it was about six feet long and two and a half feet in diameter, giving ample room for a man stretched out at full length. It was cylindrical in shape, and iron hoops inside and out reinforced it against the pressure of the water. One end was removable to permit the operator to enter the chamber. Once he settled in, an assistant bolted the end tightly back in place. The operator could look out through a glass viewport, about four inches across, in the floor beneath his face.

There were two holes for his arms to pass through, and tightly laced leather sleeves kept the water from leaking in around his arms.

The chamber was suspended from a vessel on the surface, so that it could easily be moved from place to place. The operator signaled to his surface crew by tugging on a line, as divers often do today. Lethbridge reported that he could maneuver this diving chamber over an area of twelve feet by twelve feet at the bottom (about as big as an ordinary room), and could stay down for thirty-four minutes. When the air began to get bad, he had himself hauled up, and an assistant pumped fresh air into the chamber with a bellows.

Ten fathoms (sixty feet) was his usual working limit, but he occasionally went down as far as twelve fathoms (seventy-two feet). The additional twelve feet of depth caused Lethbridge great difficulty, perhaps because of the effects of the increased pressure and cold on his arms and hands.

To judge from the number of documents that mention him, Lethbridge's services were much in demand. He made hundreds of dives, some in such faraway places as the West Indies and the Cape of Good Hope. Even foreign governments sought him out, and the French once hired him to salvage a cargo of coins from a ship sunk in the harbor of Marseilles, in the south of France.

In the years following Lethbridge's success, a number of other men attempted to build undersea vehicles. Two are worth mentioning here. One was designed in 1772 by a French nobleman named the Sieur de Dionis. Like Drebbel, he used a chemical solution to purify the air and make re-breathing it possible. Eyewitnesses report that he took ten passengers across the broad mouth of the Gironde River completely submerged. The trip took four and one half hours. Considering that the mouth of the Gironde is about six miles across at its widest point, this was not bad speed for a man-powered craft, and it was a real test for his air-purifying system.

John Day, an English shipyard carpenter, was not as fortunate as the Sieur de Dionis. In fact, his experiments ended in tragedy. Day was an uneducated man. He was described by someone who knew him well as illiterate, gloomy, peevish, and stingy. Along with these unlikable qualities he seems also to have had intelligence and a strong streak of stubborn determination. This bulldog streak of stubbornness, however, was to prove his undoing.

Day began experimenting with a series of models. Then, in 1772 or 1773, he built a small boat in which he is said to have submerged to a depth of thirty feet for twelve hours. Encouraged by this success, Day determined to try for bigger things. Since Day was a mere workingman, he had no money to spare for such a venture. Yet, somehow, he managed to coax well-to-do enthusiasts into contributing a total of 340 pounds. With these funds he bought a fifty-ton sloop and converted it into a submersible. He removed the masts—useless underwater—and constructed a large air chamber amidships. In this he installed seventy-five hogsheads filled with air. The rest of the hull was used for holding ballast.

Day's plan was to load the hull with ballast, although not enough to sink it. The

In this sturdy-looking craft John Day gambled with his life.

weight needed for submerging was to be supplied by huge nets full of stones, hung from the hull in such a way that Day could release them from inside. The built-in buoyancy of the watertight hull would then float the craft swiftly to the surface. Day made a successful trial dive in shallow water, then resolved to make a really deep dive farther out.

At some point, Day, always in need of money, contacted a notorious gambler named Christopher Blake. Blake agreed to give Day a 10-percent cut of every thousand pounds he could win by betting that Day could make the descent to the bottom and return safely to the surface. To make the odds more attractive, Day was pledged to submerge to 100 feet and remain under for twelve hours. While he was submerged, Blake's agents were to go through the crowd of spectators, taking additional bets.

On June 20, 1774, everything was in readiness. The boat, now painted bright red, was towed out to the appointed spot for the dive. On top of the hull were tied a number of colored floats, which Day was to release as signals. The inventor entered the air compartment with a candle and a supply of biscuits. Under the eyes of the expectant crowd, he was sealed in, and ballast was loaded on. But the boat refused to sink. Day called out for more stones, which were hastily tossed in. At last the boat sank beneath the surface, quickly disappearing from sight in the chilly, gray water of the English Channel. It came to rest at 22 fathoms (132 feet).

The hours dragged by, but, ominously, no colored signal floats appeared. At the time scheduled for Day's return, he did not surface. A rescue party was ordered out from a nearby navy dockyard, and the crew of the warship H.M.S. *Orpheus* was also assigned to the search. They failed to make any contact with the sunken vessel. Later, a London doctor tried to drag the bottom with grappling irons, in the unrealistic hope of bringing up the wreck and restoring the drowned inventor to life. He hooked into the wreck, but stormy weather prevented him from raising it, and the project had to be abandoned. Since the boat was never recovered, no one knows exactly what happened to Day. Probably the hull collapsed under the pressure of the water, and Day, trapped inside, drowned.

Only a few years after John Day's tragic

disappearance, a submersible was navigated successfully. The scene was New York harbor, a quarter of the way around the world from England; the year, 1776. The submersible was a most unboatlike-looking craft designed by a young New Englander named David Bushnell. Its mission was war.

Bushnell was born on an out-of-the-way farm in the township of Saybrook, Connecticut, about 1742. He stayed on the farm, helping out with the work and avoiding contact with people, until his father died. Then, at the age of twenty-seven, Bushnell sold his share of the farm and used the money to prepare for college. He entered Yale in the fall of 1771, graduating in 1775. During his freshman year at Yale, Bushnell made a significant experiment. An instructor had stated that gunpowder would not explode underwater. Bushnell, doubting him, decided to see for himself. And so he fashioned a waterproof container which he packed with gunpowder and a firing device. He found that, not only would the gunpowder go off underwater, but its force was greatly increased, since the density of the water kept the force of the explosion from being dissipated.

This suggested to Bushnell the possibility of constructing explosive mines, or bombs, to be attached to the keels of warships. There was an obvious difficulty to this scheme, however: How to get the mines in place? A swimmer could be too easily detected. A surface boat was even easier to spot. The answer was a boat that could travel underwater.

In 1775 Bushnell built a submersible which he called *The American Turtle,*

possibly because it could travel underwater, and possibly because its shape (as he said) reminded him of two turtle shells stuck together belly to belly. He built the odd-looking craft in Saybrook and tested it in the nearby Connecticut River.

At this point, relations between the American Colonies and Great Britain were extremely tense. Although independence had not yet been declared, fighting had broken out, and a kind of partial state of war existed. To keep the British from finding out about the weapon he was designing, Bushnell had to carry out the construction and testing in secrecy—no easy task in a New England village where everyone knew his neighbors' business.

It is not clear how much Bushnell knew about the work of earlier submersible designers, but the *Turtle* was a truly advanced craft for its time. It contained features never before used, but found today in the most modern submersibles.

No exact description of the *Turtle* was ever written—not even by Bushnell—so historians have drawn rather different-looking versions of it. However, most of them do agree that from the side the *Turtle* looked more or less egg-shaped, with the small end of the "egg" at the bottom. From the front, it looked like Bushnell's image of two turtle shells. A massive lead weight at the bottom kept the little craft balanced upright. Only six feet high, it could hold one man and enough air for thirty minutes of submersion.

The one-man crew entered the *Turtle* through a hatch at the top. Once inside, he sat on a seat much like a modern bicycle seat and cranked a screw-shaped propeller by hand. The *Turtle* had two propellers,

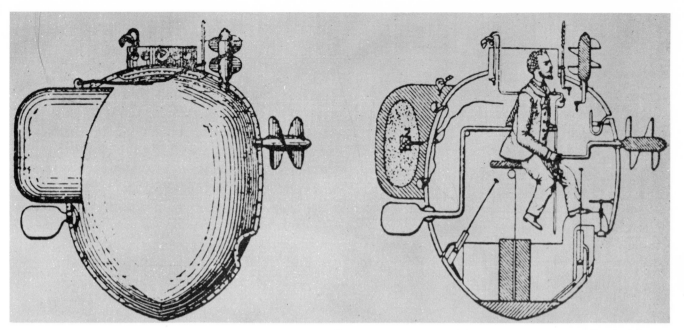

Bushnell's American Turtle, *as drawn by a U.S. Navy officer in 1885. No drawings by Bushnell himself survived.*

one to drive it forward or backward, the other to maneuver it up or down in the water. This is the first known use of a propeller to drive a boat of any kind. There were also a rudder and two pumps, possibly foot-powered, for getting rid of water.

To submerge, the operator used one foot to press a pedal that admitted water to a ballast tank. When the vessel had reached the delicately balanced state of neutral buoyancy, neither sinking nor rising, he cut off the flow of water and maneuvered it down with the vertical propeller. If he made the ballast too heavy, he emptied a little out with his pumps. To rise to the surface, he pumped the ballast tank empty.

The *Turtle* cruised with its top end just above the surface. The operator looked out through the viewports of a low conning tower, which, Bushnell said, resembled a large brass hat. Two ventilating tubes protruded from the top, one to admit fresh air and the other to let out stale air. Flaps automatically closed the ventilating tubes

when a wave broke over them or when the vessel submerged. The idea was to cruise along the surface as close to the enemy as possible, then submerge to avoid detection. Once submerged, the operator could tell from a pressure-operated depth gauge (invented by Bushnell) how deep he was, and a compass gave him his direction. (He had taken a compass bearing on his target before submerging.) The eerie glow of phosphorus lighted these instruments as the operator made his way through the water. There was no periscope (it would not be invented for many years), which was another reason the operator stayed at the surface as long as possible.

Once beneath the keel of the enemy ship, the *Turtle's* operator would attach the explosive mine that was carried on the back of the boat. This, too, was an amazing piece of engineering. The mine contained 150 pounds of gunpowder, along with a clockwork mechanism to set it off. Working from the inside of the *Turtle,* the operator was supposed to attach the mine by twisting a large screw into the planking of the enemy ship. This done, he was to back off rapidly, leaving the mine behind. A short rope held the mine to the screw embedded in the enemy ship. Being lighter than water, the mine would float up and nestle snugly next to the hull. The action of releasing the mine set the firing mechanism going. While the clockwork ticked its way toward explosion, the operator had time to make his escape.

Bushnell demonstrated his invention to the governor of Connecticut and other Revolutionary leaders; George Washington took an interest in it. They were impressed enough to place money, munitions, and manpower at Bushnell's disposal.

In 1776 the *Turtle* had its first trial in combat. A large British fleet was blockading New York harbor, as part of a plan to gain control of the Hudson River and cut New England off from the rest of the colonies. It was decided that the *Turtle* should attempt to blow up the flagship of the British fleet, the fifty-gun frigate H.M.S. *Eagle*. Bushnell himself, although a brilliant inventor, was no seaman. Furthermore, he was not strong enough to propel the *Turtle* himself. Instead, he had to recruit and train others to operate his unconventional and complicated little craft.

The first recruit developed into an expert operator, but he was taken sick before he had an opportunity to engage the enemy, and never recovered enough strength to crank the *Turtle* through the water by hand. Second choice was a young army sergeant, Ezra Lee. After a hasty training, Lee was towed close to the British fleet under cover of darkness. He

submerged and propelled the *Turtle* under the towering stern of the *Eagle*. As instructed, he turned the rod that held the wood screw. But it would not bite into the *Eagle*'s hull. Lee had struck metal—perhaps the copper sheathing that protected the bottoms of British ships against the destructive borings of shipworms; perhaps one of the iron straps that supported the rudder. (Bushnell insisted afterward that it must have been the iron rudder strap, since his screw was supposed to penetrate copper as well as wood.)

Now a strong tide set in, making it difficult for Lee to hold the *Turtle* in position, and the air inside was becoming exhausted. Lee had to surface in order to get fresh air. But daylight was fast coming on, and patrolling British guard boats noticed the odd object floating in the water. The alarm was given, and Lee hastily submerged, releasing the mine in the hope that it would come to rest against a British ship before it blew up. Because water in the harbor was choppy, making pursuit difficult, Lee escaped. Meanwhile, the clockwork firing mechanism did its job, and the mine went off with a roar. No one was killed or wounded, however, and no damage was reported. But the British were now on their guard against this sort of attack on their ships.

Some weeks later, another attempt was made to sink a British ship farther up the Hudson River. This time Lee lost track of his target while submerged, and by the time he worked his way back, the tide swept him away. In the fall, the *Turtle* was sunk by cannon fire while being carried in a surface boat. Bushnell recovered it, but it was never sent into action again.

It is believed that it was eventually dismantled to keep it out of British hands and never put back together.

Bushnell invented several other devices for sinking British ships. Once he packed a number of kegs with gunpowder and let them float down the Delaware River with the current. This time, the target was the British fleet guarding Philadelphia. Again, the attack was to be made under cover of darkness. However, neither Bushnell nor his local contact man was familiar with the river, and they launched the kegs too far upstream. It was a cold December night, and the kegs were held up by ice. By the time they worked free, it was daylight, and they were clearly visible to the British. One was hauled into a boat for investigation and exploded. The British, now alerted, stationed troops on both banks of the river and blazed away at every floating object. This "battle of the kegs" became a favorite story among Americans, and it was even made into a humorous song.

Unable to continue his experiments with torpedoes because the British were now too suspicious, Bushnell joined the army as an engineering officer. After the war, he served briefly as commander of the Corps of Engineers at West Point, but resigned from that post. For the next ten or twelve years, it was thought that he was in France and had died there, but he reappeared in Georgia in 1795, teaching school under the name of Dr. Bush. Later, he practiced medicine, which he continued until his death at the age of eighty-four. It is thought that he masqueraded under this assumed name because the public detested submarines and exploding mines as dirty weapons. And they did not like men who invented them.

Although the *Turtle* never accomplished its military missions, the little egg-shaped craft performed admirably in all other respects. Bushnell pioneered in the use of the screw propeller, the conning tower, the depth gauge, and the first crude versions of the torpedo. He may also have been the first to navigate underwater by instruments. His success, limited as it was, inspired other men. Although the *Turtle* was designed to submerge only a few feet, it was the direct ancestor of the deep submersible as we know it today.

5

The First "Nautilus"

DESPITE its lack of military success, word of Bushnell's *Turtle* may have spread to Europe. At any rate, in the closing years of the eighteenth century several Frenchmen developed plans for military submarines. None of these was practical—one even called for flapping underwater wings that would be powered by a steam engine. The resistance of the water would have made the wings useless, even if a steam engine light and powerful enough for the task had existed then—which it did not. But a young American named Robert Fulton was visiting France, and he was trying to promote the idea of a submarine. Although Fulton is best known today for his work with steamboats, his real interest lay in underwater navigation. He considered his steamboats merely a way of making money.

Fulton was born near Lancaster, Pennsylvania, in 1765. His father, a well-to-do tailor in Lancaster, had retired from his business and bought a large farm not long before Robert was born. The farm was on bad land, however, and the family sank into poverty. Unable to pay their debts, they lost the farm. A few years later, the father died.

As a schoolboy, Robert was fascinated with painting. He was apprenticed to an artist in Philadelphia, and by the time he was seventeen, he was earning money from his paintings. At the age of twenty-two, aided by some of the wealthy and important people for whom he had done pictures, he went off to England to study under a famous American-born artist named Benjamin West.

Fulton was an ambitious young man, and he had a knack for making friends with rich and powerful people who could help him get ahead. It did not hurt his chances that he was also found handsome,

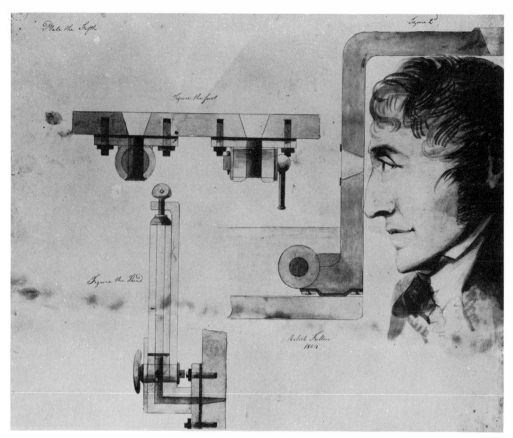

Robert Fulton drew this portrait of himself testing a viewing device he invented.

charming, and brilliant. However, he was not a good enough artist to make a success in England, and so he turned to mechanical inventions and to planning canal systems. It happened that England already had plenty of canals, and no one was interested in his inventions. So, in 1796, he decided to try his luck in France. England and France had been officially at war since 1793, but a good many civilians passed back and forth by way of neutral countries. One of them was an American named Joel Barlow, a rich, well-known writer, equipped with excellent political connections. Fulton and Barlow became close friends. Barlow had been at Yale while Bushnell was there, and he had also been a friend of one of the men who had worked most closely with Bushnell during the Revolutionary War. It is likely that Fulton thought of building a submarine from

hearing Barlow talk about Bushnell's *American Turtle*. (Fulton never admitted this. To the very end of his life he insisted that he had conceived the idea of a submarine by himself.)

Near the end of 1797 Fulton wrote to the French government, offering to build what he called "a mechanical *Nautulus*" (his spelling), that is, a submarine, to destroy the British fleet. In so doing, he said, he would bring freedom to the seas. Nations would be able to trade peaceably with each other, unhindered by the armed fleets of selfish rulers. For his part in bringing peace and freedom to the seas, Fulton asked a stiff price. He wanted a monopoly on building submarines, a large bounty on each British warship that he sank, and the right to keep as a prize of war every ship that he captured. (At that time private citizens were allowed to outfit and operate their own armed raiders under a government license. Under this arrangement, the government was spared the expense of building and manning a warship, and the privateer, as the owner of the vessel was called, was allowed to keep all the ships and cargoes that he captured. If these *prizes*, as they were termed, were sold, the money was split between the owner and the crew. The more enemy vessels captured, the more money earned. Eventually privateering, which was actually a kind of legalized piracy, got so out of hand that it was abolished by international agreement in 1856. In Fulton's day, however, it flourished.)

In case the French government did not wish to grant him these enormously profitable terms, Fulton suggested an alternative: the government should build the boats according to his design, and pay him a royalty fee equal to about $20,000 on each one. As prices went in those days, Fulton could have retired comfortably for the rest of his life on the royalty from just one submarine.

Quite understandably, the French government rejected Fulton's exorbitant demands. They were seriously interested in his idea for a submarine, however. They bargained hard about the price, but in the end turned the project down. The reason was that Fulton, fearing reprisals against his crewmen if they were captured, insisted that they be given government commissions and the promise of official protection. This the French were unwilling to do. Said the French Minister of Marine (naval minister), "It is not possible to grant commissions to men who make use of such means to destroy the enemy's forces."

The French did not want to take the blame for blowing up ships or encouraging a foreign terrorist.

Months passed, and the Minister of Marine was replaced by a new man. Fulton submitted his proposal once again. This time, the government appointed a panel of distinguished scientists to consider the invention, and Fulton constructed a clockwork-driven model for them. In some respects it was like Bushnell's *Turtle,* in others quite different. The design of the explosive mine and the method he proposed for attaching it were almost exactly like Bushnell's. He also kept the screw-shaped propeller and the conning tower, but he gave the hull a long, cigarlike shape like that of a modern submarine. He also proposed to use diving planes, flaps like the elevator flaps of an airplane, to steer his submersible down and up, rather than a vertical propeller like the *Turtle*'s.

Like all submersibles up to this point, the *Nautilus* was to be hand-powered. To increase her speed and cruising range, Fulton proposed to use two or three sailors to turn the hand cranks. For long-distance cruising on the surface, he designed an ingenious collapsible sail and mast that could quickly be folded up and stowed in a groove on the submersible's upper deck.

The French scientists on the panel were very much impressed by Fulton's ideas, but they had some criticisms. They pointed out that the boat would not move fast enough underwater to make diving planes work; so he changed to a vertical propeller. They told him that the spiral screw he used as a propeller in the model would not work well on a full-sized boat; so he designed a four-bladed propeller of the modern type. He also added ventilating tubes and the depth gauge that Bushnell had invented. With a few more modifications, the panel strongly recommended that the government give Fulton the money he needed to build his submarine. Instead of following the advice of its experts, the government did nothing. So Fulton had an English friend carry reports of his invention to Britain, hoping that the British government would hear of it. They did indeed, but the British were not prepared to move at this point.

With no money coming in, Fulton had to do something, so he took out a patent on the idea of the panorama, a tremendous picture, illustrating some dramatic event, which was painted on the inside of an enormous dome. He put up a building in Paris and around the inside he painted the city of Moscow being destroyed by flames (this had happened a good many years ago, but people were still talking about it). The panorama was an instant hit, and the money from admission fees poured in. With these profits, plus funds that he wheedled out of private backers, Fulton was able to build a submarine on his own.

He had the *Nautilus* built at the workshop of France's biggest manufacturer of steam engines, because they had the best facilities for the kind of metal construction he desired. Fulton did not rely on wood alone in the building of his submersible. The planks of the hull were sheathed in copper, and an inner framework of iron added strength against the pressure of the water. Noted French scientists helped with their advice as construction progressed.

Completed, the *Nautilus* looked rather

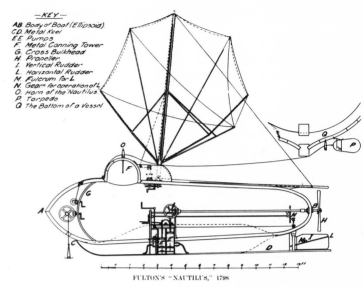

—KEY—
A B. Body of Boat (Ellipsoid)
C D. Metal Keel
E E. Pumps
F. Metal Conning Tower
G. Cross Bulkhead
H. Propeller
I. Vertical Rudder
L. Horizontal Rudder
M. Fulcrum for L
N. Gears for operation of L
O. Horn of the 'Nautilus'
P. Torpedo
Q. The Bottom of a Vessel

FULTON'S "NAUTILUS," 1798

A diagram of Fulton's Nautilus, *showing the propulsion mechanism and the folding sail for travel on the surface.*

like a fat cigar with a hump—the conning tower—at one end. It was twenty-one feet long and seven feet in diameter. The inside diameter was about six feet, which would have been quite spacious, but the hand-powered machinery for propulsion took up a good deal of the room.

The newly built *Nautilus* had its first trial in the Seine River at Rouen in the summer of 1800. Scientists and government officials were among the crowd that watched anxiously for Fulton's daring creation to surface. At last a metal hump broke through the water; a hatch opened; and out stepped the confident Fulton, followed by two sailors who had provided his motive power. They all appeared normal, a reassuring sign, although they had been submerged for forty-five minutes.

Fulton made numerous trial dives at Rouen and at the famous seaport city of Le Havre, at the mouth of the Seine. Each time some weakness in design showed up, he corrected it. He also added a spherical copper tank for compressed air to increase the breathing supply, making it possible to stay submerged longer. He made descents to twenty-five feet, which he considered the maximum limit of safety for his craft, carrying candles to read his instruments by.

In the fall of 1800 Fulton at last got the official French protection he had sought, and he set out to destroy two British warships that were blockading Le Havre. The *Nautilus* sailed out to a little island harbor a few miles from where the warships were stationed. For several weeks, storms prevented him from doing anything. When calmer weather came, Fulton and his two assistants, under cover of night, sailed as close to the enemy as they dared. Then they folded the sail and mast down into their storage groove, closed the hatch, and submerged. While the two sailors strained at the cranks, Fulton steered toward the target, guided only by his compass. As they moved slowly ahead, the tide changed. The *Nautilus* could make no headway against the current. All they could do was wait until the tide changed again. Fulton let down the anchor and ordered the crew to raise the breathing tubes. There they sat for six hours hunched up in the chilly darkness, waiting for the tide to turn in their favor. Before they reached their targets, however, the British ships hoisted their sails and moved out of range. British spies had done their work well—the commanders of the British ships had been warned.

The next year, Fulton had the *Nautilus* rebuilt at the big port of Brest (some his-

torians say that he built a second submersible). He tested it against a sloop provided by the French government. For this experiment Fulton used a mine containing only twenty pounds of gunpowder. He submerged 650 feet from the anchored sloop. As he wrote afterwards:

"Taking my direction so as to pass near the Sloop I struck her with the bomb on my Passage the explosion took place and the Sloop was torn into Atoms, in fact nothing was left but the buye [buoy] and cable, And the concussion was so Great that a Column of Water Smoak and the fibres of the Sloop was cast from 80 to 100 feet in Air." (The spelling and punctuation are Fulton's own.)

The French admiral who observed the test was horrified. After reading his report, French naval men agreed that this was a detestable weapon that no civilized nation would use. To get around the opposition of the navy, Fulton tried to go right to the top, to Napoleon himself. Napoleon, who was soon to have himself officially declared Emperor of France, had taken an intense personal dislike to the pushy foreigner who was forever lecturing him on how to run his country. Nevertheless, he listened while Fulton proposed a new idea: to have his submarine lay a barrage of floating mines across the entrances of English harbors.

The idea appealed to Napoleon, but he knew that to reach the English coast undetected by British patrol ships, the *Nautilus* would have to cross the Channel underwater. Not being sure that the little submersible was equal to a trip of this length, he told Fulton that he wished to inspect it

The Nautilus, *rebuilt with a conventional sailboat hull, is shown on the surface and submerged. Drawing may be Fulton's own.*

personally. The inventor wrote back that he had destroyed the *Nautilus,* since it leaked badly and was "but an imperfect engine." He added that he had plans for a much superior submersible, but he refused to show them to anyone connected with the government until he had been paid in advance. Napoleon, exasperated, shouted that Fulton was a charlatan and a swindler.

It was a good time for Fulton to leave France, and his intrigues with the British had finally had a result. After months of negotiations carried on through secret agents, Fulton left for England, where the government had promised him a job designing mines and torpedoes to use against the French. In fact, the British disliked the idea of underwater weapons intensely, and their real aim was to prevent Fulton from aiding the French any further.

In England, Fulton designed torpedoes to be towed by submerged catamarans, paddled by sailors dressed and masked in black so as not to show up against the night. A few days after one of his torpedo squads had made an ineffectual attack against some French ships, Horatio Nelson crushed the French fleet at the battle of Trafalgar. The British no longer had need of submarines or torpedoes. In 1806 Fulton slunk back to America, where he tried unsuccessfully to interest President Jefferson in his submarine inventions.

Although Fulton had not been able to make the submarine into a really effective military weapon, owing to the difficulty of getting his torpedoes and mines into place, he made it into a highly maneuverable craft, capable of extended underwater operations and dives of several hours' length. The blade-type propeller in itself was a major technical advance, and Fulton seems to have been the first to use it. It gave the *Nautilus* an underwater speed of two and one half miles an hour—not a bad speed for a two-manpower craft. Some modern research submersibles powered by electric motors do not go much faster.

No practical advances were made for more than forty years, although many impractical plans for submersibles were proposed. In 1845, however, a French inventor named Dr. Payerne built a diving boat specifically designed for underwater construction work. This was the first practical nonmilitary submersible (Lethbridge's vessel was a diving chamber), and it was one of the ancestors of today's research and working submersibles. One of its most interesting features was an airlock compartment that permitted divers to leave and enter to do their work without flooding the boat. It performed successfully the task of removing underwater rocks from the harbors of Brest and Cherbourg.

Payerne apparently meant to propel this submarine by a steam engine, using a chemical fuel that contained its own oxygen supply. However, it did not work, or, as a French historian tactfully put it, "it did not give the results that the inventor expected." So Payerne returned to hand propulsion.

In 1848, war broke out between Denmark and Germany. At that time, Ger-

many was not yet one country, but a loose union of independent kingdoms and dukedoms, most of them small and feeble. So at first the Danes were a match for the Germans, and Danish warships blockaded the north German coast. A Bavarian cavalry corporal named Wilhelm Bauer (Bavaria was one of the biggest and most powerful German kingdoms) tried to break the Danish blockade by means of a submarine.

The boat he designed was short, stubby, and deep, looking rather like a sardine can flattened at each end. He named it *Brandtaucher,* meaning "Surf Diver." It is thought that Bauer was trying to duplicate the shape of a porpoise to reduce the resistance of the water, but that the workers who built the boat did not understand what he was trying to do and insisted on changing the design. To get the boat built at all, Bauer had to let them have their way.

The boat was built rather hastily of sheet iron, for iron was now plentiful and cheap enough to use in shipbuilding, due to improved smelting methods. The metal hull was a step forward. Stronger and less bulky than a wooden hull, it leaves more room for the crew and machinery inside. This is especially important in a vessel as cramped for space as a submersible.

The propulsion system was two sailors turning flywheels geared to the propeller, for muscle power was still the only system

A party of well-dressed visitors, obviously not workmen, inspects the mechanism of Dr. Payerne's underwater work boat.

that worked. There was no conning tower, but two large, square windows on each side admitted light.

To submerge, the *Brandtaucher* flooded its ballast tanks in the conventional fashion, but Bauer had devised a new system for steering it up and down. This was a heavy weight which ran along a threaded rod on the floor of the boat. To dive, a crewman spun gearwheels to turn the rod, which then screwed the weight forward, tilting the nose of the submarine down. To rise, the weight was screwed back, tilting the nose up. It was a beautifully simple system, but it could go wrong with distressing ease, as Bauer later discovered.

The *Brandtaucher* went out on its first mission, in the harbor of Kiel, in December 1850. At the sight of the ungainly craft, the Danish blockade fleet scattered, for the power of torpedoes was now well respected. Encouraged by this partial success, Bauer made a second try early in 1851. Out into the harbor glided the iron surf diver, as Bauer's two husky assistants enthusiastically heaved at their cranks. Bauer gave the order to submerge, and the diving weight clanked forward along its track in the floor plates. But the angle of the dive was too steep, and the boat plunged downward nose first. Before Bauer and his crew could work the weight back, the *Brandtaucher* struck bottom, bounced, and settled right side up in sixty feet of water. The flimsy sheet iron of the hull gave way, and water leaked in with threatening speed.

The machinery had been knocked out of place by the force of the crash; so the boat could not be moved. Nor could Bauer clear the ballast tanks with compressed air,

because the equipment was so badly damaged. The men could not budge the escape hatch against the pressure of the water. As a last resort, Bauer ordered them to flood the interior of the submarine, hoping in this way to compress the air trapped in the hull until its pressure equaled that of the surrounding water.

As a German news reporter described the accident:

The sailors, who up till now had shown great courage in their ignorance, did not understand Bauer's orders, refused to obey, and even began to abuse him. He in his turn began to abuse them, and it was only by threats and entreaties that he managed to convince the men that it was the only way to save their lives. They started again to work by the dim light that came through the portholes. . . . After a great many efforts and anxieties, chiefly caused by the men on the surface throwing anchors and grapnels which threatened to destroy their portholes, the water entering compressed the air in the interior of the boat to such an extent that it burst open the weakly constructed hatches, with the result that Bauer and his two companions were shot up to the surface like corks out of a champagne bottle.

They had been trapped on the bottom for five hours.

Bauer was unable to interest any of the German governments in financing any more experiments with submersibles, so he turned next to Britain, whose Queen Victoria had a German husband, Prince Albert. The prince was not only friendly toward fellow Germans but was also keenly interested in science and technology.

Prince Albert supplied Bauer with

money and brought him together with three of Britain's leading ship designers. One of Britain's most popular and colorful political leaders, Lord Palmerston, also took a hand in the project of designing British submarines. Unfortunately, the Bavarian cavalry corporal did not get along with his new, aristocratic colleagues, and, after they had milked him of his ideas and plans, they told him genteelly that he was no longer needed. A submarine was subsequently built from a British modification of Bauer's plans. It went to the bottom with its crew.

Bauer applied to the United States and found no interest there. But in Russia, which was then involved in the Crimean War against Turkey, Britain, and France, he found a customer. The Russian fleet was far outclassed by the up-to-date warships of Britain and France. Perhaps Russia's leaders hoped that a fleet of submarines would equalize the odds.

So in 1856 Bauer built for the Russians a submarine twice as large as the *Brandtaucher,* fifty-two feet long and twelve feet wide. Its propeller was driven by a treadmill, an endless belt fitted with cleats, on which men walked to turn a power shaft. A unique feature was a pair of long, heavy rubber gloves extending through holes in the bow. A crewman could put his hands and arms into these to release the 500-pound bomb the vessel carried, attach it to an enemy ship, and trigger the firing mechanism. Thus, the gloves made it possible for a person inside the protective hull of a submersible to perform work outside the hull. Some modern submersibles have mechanical work arms, a refinement of Bauer's idea.

This submarine, called the *Diable Marin* (French for *Sea Devil*), was never tested in combat, for the fighting was over before the ship was completed. However, it is believed that Bauer made over a hundred successful dives in it, conducting examinations of the harbor floor and experimenting with the behavior of sound underwater. In the fall of 1856, on the coronation day of the new Tsar, Alexander II, he submerged with four musicians. When cannon overhead boomed out the signal that the crown had been placed on the tsar's head, the band struck up the Russian national anthem. The music could be heard plainly by people aboard the ships in the harbor.

Despite this patriotic performance, the Russian officers with whom he worked disliked the German foreigner. They nicknamed him "Little Corporal" by way of comparing him sarcastically with Napoleon, and they sneered at his lower-class lack of manners. Some historians think that they even tried to sabotage him, for on one dive they gave him inaccurate information about the depth of the bottom, and the *Sea Devil* got stuck in a mudbank. Although the submarine was finally extricated, and no lives were lost, it was several weeks before Bauer was able to repair all the damage. Not long afterward, the boat sank.

Bauer had bad luck throughout his life. When he turned from submarines to salvage work, the ship he had just raised sank again in a violent storm. He died in poverty in Munich, his only income a small government pension. After his death the government erected a monument to him, and the *Brandtaucher,* fished up from the bottom of Kiel harbor, was put on exhibition—too late to help its inventor.

In 1851—the same year in which the *Brandtaucher* went down—an American shoemaker named Lodner Philips launched a forty-foot submersible in Lake Michigan. When the submarine was running just below the surface, it could get air from a short, telescoping air tube, and for deep dives the air breathed by the crew was passed through a system of water sprays to absorb carbon dioxide, enabling it to be breathed over and over. It is said that Philips once took his wife and two children on a dive that lasted for an entire day and had enough air left over to supply four people for six hours.

In the bow of the boat was a watertight, ball-shaped joint in a sliding frame. By means of this device, a person inside the boat could operate a saw, grab tongs, and other tools mounted outside the hull. Two men turned the propeller by muscle power, reaching a reported speed of four miles per hour. A pendulum-operated device automatically kept the boat on an even keel. Philips claimed that he could also keep the boat perfectly steady at any depth down to two hundred feet, and that he had sawed through fourteen-inch timbers underwater. These claims were never proved, however.

He planned to install a steam engine, but did not carry out this plan, for he was lost with his vessel during a dive in Lake Erie. It is thought that he went too deep, and the boat was crushed under the pressure.

The first power-driven submersible was built in 1853. To be precise, it was a large semisubmersible gunboat, running with the top of its hull awash but never going completely below the surface. The inventor was James Nasmyth, a Scot who had invented a number of steam-powered machines for ironworking. Nasmyth called the ship a "floating mortar." The newspapers nicknamed it a "water hog." The floating mortar was eighty feet long and thirty feet wide. Its sides, built of soft poplar wood, were ten feet thick. A cannonball could sink into these soft, thick sides with very little damage to the ship. In the nose, which was armored with a heavy brass cap that could double as a ram, sat a heavy mortar designed for firing underwater. A steam engine pushed the floating mortar slowly along, with only a small conning tower and a stubby smokestack showing above the surface. Approaching an enemy ship within a few feet, the "water hog" was to sink her with a mortar shell below the waterline. The "water hog" was never used, and when Nasmyth wrote his autobiography he passed over it discreetly. However, it was a historic step toward applying power to submersible craft.

Interest in submersibles was growing with each advance in technology. Had a major war broken out in Europe, submersible design might have taken a great leap forward. As it was, the American Civil War would soon give it impetus.

Nearly submerged, James Nasmyth's unsuccessful "water hog" steams at an enemy ship in this completely imaginary scene.

6

Military Submarines:
Trials and Errors

WHEN the Civil War broke out in 1861, the North placed a blockade along the coast of the South, cutting off badly needed supplies from Europe and also preventing the South from shipping cotton out in exchange for cash and weapons. The Confederate States Navy was too weak to break the blockade. Swift, nimble blockade-runner ships were able to sneak through the Union blockade with distressing frequency, but they were built for speed and could not carry enough cargo to make a real difference. The Confederates, finding the North a far tougher antagonist than they had imagined, turned in desperation to submarine warfare.

A series of submersibles and semisubmersibles, all named *David*, was built in Southern dockyards. The name was taken from the Bible story of David, the shepherd boy who fought and killed the fearsome giant Goliath.

The first recorded attack by a Southern submersible took place off Charleston, South Carolina, in 1863. This *David* was about fifty feet long and nine feet in diameter. It must have been at most a semisubmersible, for it was powered by a steam engine, and steam engines were not practical for a boat that submerged completely. In the last faint light of an October evening, the *David,* decks awash and going slowly so as not to reveal its presence by sparks from the smokestack, steamed toward its target, the Union ironclad *New Ironsides.* From the bow protruded a long spar carrying a torpedo at its end. The South had learned, from the failures of Fulton and Bushnell, not to place torpedoes by hand. Now, torpedoes were to be rammed into place by the full weight of the attack boat. A spike on the end of the torpedo would pierce copper sheathing and ship's timbers (even ironclads were not usually

46

Sketched by a contemporary newspaper artist, a Confederate David *rests on the beach.*

armored below the waterline), holding the torpedo in place while a time fuse delayed the explosion until the attack boat backed off to safety.

Lookouts aboard the *New Ironsides* sensed that something was approaching them in the darkness. They dimly made out a mass that looked at first like floating logs, but they soon realized it was not. Could it be a Confederate ram? The cannons on the Union ironclad could not be aimed at such a low-lying target so close by, so the ship's marines were ordered to fire on the enemy with their carbines, in the vain hope of repelling the attacker that way. The *David*'s crew lined up on their own deck to snipe at the defenders. On came the almost invisible submersible, hitting its target squarely in the side. There was a great, boiling explosion, and the *New Ironsides* rolled far over with the force of the blow. The *David* leaped into the air, fell back on the water, briefly submerging, and came afloat again. Two of the crew clambered back aboard the still-floating submersible and escaped into the night. The rest were taken prisoner. The

New Ironsides suffered little damage, although the psychological effect on the North was considerable.

The best known of the Confederate submersible designers was a naval captain named Hunley. His *David*s were hand-propelled and had slim, cigar-shaped hulls. They had to run afloat until the last possible moment, as there was no air supply for submerged operation. Hunley was not a good designer, and he was plagued by bad luck as well. His first submersible, built in New Orleans in 1862, was lost when Union forces captured the city. The second sank in a storm while being towed to a Confederate naval base. The third sank a Union ship but destroyed itself in so doing.

This *David,* often known as *Hunley* after its designer, was twenty-five feet long and powered by eight men cranking a propeller. It was so poorly designed and badly built that it sank several times before it went into action, drowning a total of thirty-five crewmen. Once the wake of a passing steamboat was enough to send it to the bottom, and once it sank at anchor. By the

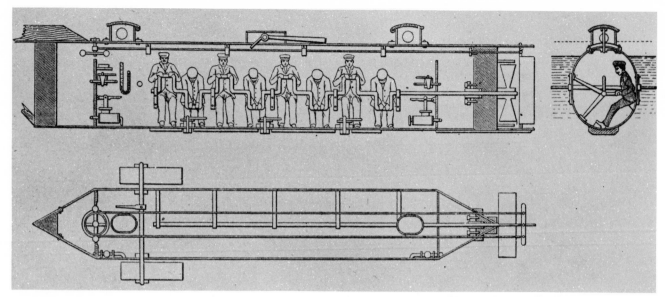

Cutaway views of Hunley's David *from side and top. View at top right shows a crewman at crank.*

time it went into battle, early in 1864, it had earned such a bad reputation that not even eight men could be found to volunteer for the crew. The *David* put out to sea shorthanded, under the inexpert command of an infantry lieutenant.

The submarine made the standard nighttime sneak attack. Its target was the Union corvette *Housatonic.* (A corvette was a small, fast warship.) Either on orders from a nervous Confederate naval command or because the crew themselves were afraid of drowning, the *David* did not submerge, but lay so low in the water that it came within 100 yards of its target before it was spotted. The crew made a final dash, rammed the torpedo firmly into the hull of the Union ship, and prepared to back off. However, the time fuse went off prematurely, and the *David* was blown up along with the *Housatonic.*

This disaster marked the end of the Confederate submersible campaign. However, it sent shock waves through the North, and European military observers, who were studying the American Civil War with keen interest, were greatly im-

pressed by the destructive capability of the submarine.

While the Civil War was being fought, other nations were not idle. About 1863, two Frenchmen designed and launched a submersible powered by compressed air. Unfortunately, the *Plongeur (Plunger),* as the boat was named, was badly designed and tended to drive itself under whenever power was applied. After a series of unsuccessful trials, marked by dangerous accidents, it was discarded. It is believed that the hull was salvaged and turned into a water tank.

An invention that had great influence on the development of submarines was the self-propelled torpedo, which was invented in 1868 and reached a practical stage by 1870. Powered by compressed air and kept on course by automatic steering fins, the self-propelled torpedo could be launched from a safe distance. No longer was it necessary to run the risks of fastening the torpedo to an enemy ship by hand, or of ramming it into the enemy's side, possibly blowing the delivery ship up in the process.

When the torpedo had proved itself in tests, governments suddenly became very interested in submarine warfare. The number of submarines invented—and even built—jumped. Consequently, some important advances were made in submarine design. The most important was the replacement of muscle power by machinery. It was becoming increasingly obvious that human muscles could not propel a submersible fast enough or far enough to do more than attack a ship lying motionless at anchor nearby. The rapidly developing technology of the later 1800s solved this problem with a variety of sources of mechanical power. Each kind of power—steam, electric, compressed air, and so on—was tried out, with many failures, until a satisfactory system was worked out toward the end of the century.

Steam was a logical first choice. The steam engine was now long past the experimental stage, and it had no "bugs" left to work out. On surface ships, the steam engine was reliable and had proved itself in daily use for over sixty years. However, it turned out to be ill suited for underwater operation. There were several reasons for this. To begin with, a steam engine needed a large and steady supply of air for the fire under its boiler. This was not available underwater. If a snorkel tube was used to provide air, there was still a problem with the terrific heat generated by the boiler. Trapped inside the metal hull of the submersible, the heat turned it into an underwater oven. Heavy insulation around the boiler and steam pipes helped somewhat, but the cramped quarters inside a submersible did not leave much room for insulation. The smoke and exhaust gases

from the fire were a third problem. If they were not led away to the surface through a smokestack, they quickly suffocated the crew. But if a smokestack was used, the smoke and steam billowing out from it made the submersible as easy to spot as a freight train. Furthermore, without special provisions in the design, a steam-powered submersible could not go deeper than the length of its snorkel tube and smokestack. And the drag of the water against the big tubes of the stack and snorkel would have slowed the sub to a crawl.

Compressed air seemed like a good alternative. It was clean, smoke free, and heatless. Unfortunately, it was used up too quickly for any sort of long-range operation. And it left a trail of bubbles that an alert lookout might spot.

Electric power reached a practical stage in the 1870s. It was clean, quiet, cool, fume free, and it left no telltale trail. But electric power was not ideal, either. The batteries were heavy and took up a great deal of space. And, though they lasted longer than compressed air, they soon ran out of power. One hundred miles was considered a good cruising range for an electric-powered submersible before its batteries ran down and had to be recharged. This was all right for guarding a harbor or a short stretch of coastline, but it left the submersible useless for any military assignments requiring extensive cruising.

The solution finally came with the development of the internal-combustion engine. (An internal-combustion engine is one that works by the burning, or combustion, of fuel directly inside the engine, instead of under a boiler outside the engine. The gasoline engine and the diesel engine are both internal-combustion engines.) In theory, the internal-combustion engine had many advantages over the steam engine. It was much lighter and, since it needed no boiler, it took up much less space. It got more useful work out of each unit of fuel, thus extending the submarine's cruising range. It could be turned off when it was not being used and be ready again for action within a few minutes after it was started, whereas a steam-powered vessel either had to keep steam up in the boiler all the time or else wait several hours to get steam up in a cold boiler.

In practice, the internal-combustion engine had some faults along with its virtues. It was liable to go out of order at inconvenient moments, and it would not always start. Like the steam engine, it needed an air supply and a means of getting rid of exhaust. This last was very important, because the exhaust of an internal-combustion engine contains large quantities of the deadly gas carbon monoxide.

By the 1880s the internal-combustion engine had become practical enough for some inventors to use it in their submarines. However, it did not really come into its own until the 1890s, when inventors began to use dual systems of propulsion: a fuel-burning engine for the surface, plus electric power for running submerged. In this way, they gained some of the advantages of both systems. And the internal-combustion engine, by now a considerably more reliable piece of machinery, worked well in this combination. It made the submarine a truly practical, long-range craft.

Periscopes came into general use to permit submarines, while underwater, to track their targets. Without a periscope, an attacking submarine had to approach its target blind, guided by its compass toward the point where the target was last seen. There was no way for the submarine commander to know whether the target had moved, nor was he able to tell how far from the target he was—unless, of course, he surfaced briefly for a look, in which case he lost his advantage of secrecy. Thus the periscope contributed to the growing acceptance of submarines by the world's navies.

As submarines became faster and more maneuverable, the problem of depth control became serious. Once in a submerged state of neutral buoyancy, where the submarine weighs the same as the volume of water it displaces, a submarine is very delicately balanced. A slight impulse is enough to make it nose down toward the depths or up toward the surface. And almost anything could disturb this delicate balance—the firing of a torpedo, the sloshing back and forth of water in a ballast tank or a boiler, or too sharp an adjustment of the diving planes, for example. Often, when changing depth, a submarine would plunge too far, then, as the helmsman tried to recover, zoom up to the surface, sometimes actually leaping partway into the air. Then down again and up again, until the wildly plunging vessel was finally brought under control. Old-time submarine men called this behavior "porpoising," and it drove them frantic, and with good reason. A submarine that went into a nose dive in shallow water often got stuck in the bottom, trapping the crew, or suffered damage to the hull and machinery. In deep water, it could go beyond the pressure limit of the hull and be crushed like an empty tin can. Even if none of these accidents happened, it was still difficult and uncomfortable for the crew to do their jobs while being tossed about.

Submarines that dived under power, using their diving planes, were particularly vulnerable to this sort of wild behavior. Some inventors therefore stuck to the old principle, used by Fulton, of submerging on a level keel, either by letting water into the ballast tanks to overcome the vessel's buoyancy or by using vertical propellers. This system, however, made for slower submersion, and in wartime a few extra seconds could make the difference between safety or destruction.

In spite of these defects, by 1900, the basic problems of power, vision, stability and depth control had either been solved or were well on the way to being solved.

Dozens of submersibles were built in the last half of the nineteenth century, and many more were planned but never constructed. Some were practical, some impractical. Men of many different nations were involved in their design.

A Russian engineer named Drzwiecki pioneered several ideas that later appeared in the submersibles of other inventors, notably a propeller that could be tilted up or down to aid in diving or rising. This feature is found on some modern research submersibles.

Drzwiecki's first submersible, built in 1876, was a small, experimental craft only sixteen feet long. The propeller was turned by bicycle pedals instead of a hand crank (the bicycle had recently become extremely popular). He named it *Podascaphe* (Greek for "foot boat"). In 1879 Drzwiecki built a larger *Podascaphe,* this time with a tilting propeller and a four-man crew. He followed it in 1884 with an electric-powered submersible, this time with a standard screw and a rudder.

In France, the most noteworthy submersible inventor was a civil engineer named Claude Goubet. As early as 1881 he constructed some small, torpedo-carrying submarines powered by four men working foot treadles like those of old-fashioned sewing machines. Russia ordered 500 of these mechanisms, to be placed in Russian-built hulls. Perhaps the reason was that manpower was cheap in Russia, while engines were expensive. In any case, it is believed that about 50 were delivered.

Drzwiecki's second Podascaphe *(1879). Drawing shows the ingenious tilting propeller for steering boat up or down.*

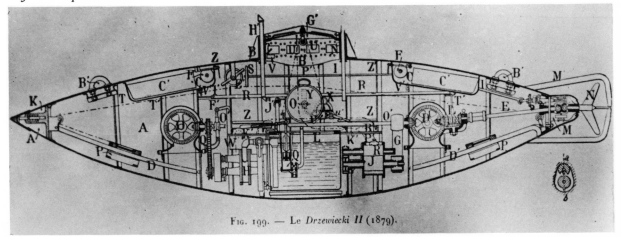

Fig. 199. — Le *Drzewiecki II* (1879).

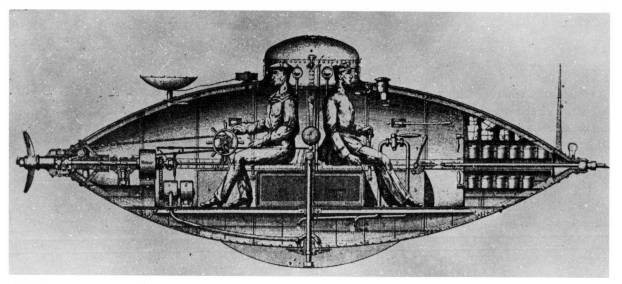

Cutaway view of the Goubet I. *Square box in center is a compressed-air tank; batteries fill the submarine's nose.*

In 1885 Goubet patented a small, electrically driven submarine. The main section of its sixteen-foot hull was cast as a single piece for added strength. It was made of bronze, which had the double advantage of resisting corrosion by seawater and of not affecting the boat's magnetic compass. The *Goubet I,* as this craft was named, had a tilting propeller and an automatic stabilizing device, regulated by a pendulum, for keeping it on an even keel. Shaped like an elongated football, it held two men, plus torpedoes with rubber suction cups carried on the outside. It was reportedly sold to Brazil for about $50,000.

In the 1890s Goubet built a larger, electric-powered submarine which he called *Goubet II.* In trials, it performed impressive feats such as cutting the anchor cables of buoys, exploding a mine, sending messages to the surface in glass floats, and doing tricky maneuvers between buoys representing mines. The French government remained unimpressed. Discouraged, Goubet eventually sold the patents on this boat to a British company. The boat itself

was sold to an amusement concern and ended its career taking tourists for brief dives in Lake Geneva, Switzerland.

In 1888 France's first official naval submarine, the *Gymnote,* was launched. This all-steel, electrically driven boat, nearly sixty feet long, was designed by an engineer named Dupuy de Lome, who died before construction could be started. A fellow naval engineer, Gustave Zédé, took charge of the plans and saw the boat through construction. Although it was unarmed and its design was experimental, the *Gymnote* was used for training submarine crews.

Gymnote was followed by two military submarines, *Gustave Zédé* and *Morse* (French for *walrus*). Both these vessels performed very badly. They were so unstable that they could hardly be controlled when they dived. Sometimes they plunged so steeply that their sterns would flip up above the surface, leaving the propeller spinning crazily in the air.

A group of engineers was called in to improve the stability of these submarines. On one observation trip they took in the

Zédé, the unpredictable craft went into a nose dive and hit bottom with such force that the experts were knocked off their seats.

Despite these discouraging performances, the French government went on to commission a large submarine named the *Narval,* which was launched in 1896. Unlike its predecessors, the *Narval* had a dual propulsion system: a steam engine for running on the surface and an electric motor for submerged operations. When on the surface, the electric motor, turned by the steam engine, served as a dynamo to recharge the batteries. Although the *Narval* was not completely successful, owing to the disadvantages of steam engines mentioned earlier, it worked well enough to keep the French building at least some steam-powered submersibles as late as 1910. And, during World War I, Britain built a number of very large steam-

powered subs that were not scrapped until the 1920s.

One of France's most important contributions was not a boat at all, but a novel: Jules Verne's *Twenty Thousand Leagues under the Sea.* First published in 1869, it became a best seller. It was translated into many languages and read all over the world.

In this book the French master of science fiction told the story of a giant submarine named the *Nautilus* (like Fulton's pioneer submersible) and its mysterious commander, Captain Nemo. Driven by an unexplained source of power that generated electricity for its powerful motors, the *Nautilus* could travel at high speed at unimaginable depths. Its crew, wearing self-contained diving suits, gathered all the food they needed from the sea. Metal ores and other natural resources also came from the sea, to be transformed by special-

The French naval submarine Gustave Zédé, *built about 1900, floats with deck awash.*

Captain Nemo, fictional hero of Jules Verne's 20,000 Leagues under the Sea, *takes his bearings from deck of the* Nautilus.

ists among the crew into tools, clothing, and other articles.

The publication of *Twenty Thousand Leagues under the Sea* had more of an effect than the launching of any actual French submersible, for the *Nautilus* fascinated the public as no real boat ever had, and it aroused worldwide interest in submersibles and undersea exploration. Furthermore, it served as the inspiration to at least one very important submarine inventor, Simon Lake.

Verne was a conscientious writer who researched his material thoroughly, and his fictional scenarios were based on the latest scientific and technical knowledge. At the time of its publication, the feats of undersea navigation described in *Twenty Thousand Leagues under the Sea* were far beyond the achievements of submersible technology. But thirty years later, by the

end of the century, they were well on their way to becoming fact.

England was the scene of a number of unsuccessful experiments with submersibles. One involved a boat named the *Nautilus,* designed in the mid-1870s by two men named Campbell and Ash. This *Nautilus* had an up-to-date electric power system, but its submergence system was based on the principles proposed by William Bourne two centuries earlier. On either side of the hull were four cylinders, which could slide in or out to reduce or expand the volume of the boat. When the cylinders were retracted, the boat lost buoyancy and sank; when they were pushed outward, buoyancy was increased, and the boat floated. At a trial demonstration, the cylinders were retracted and the *Nautilus* sank smoothly. But it refused to surface. It had settled into a layer of soft mud on the bottom, and the cylinders could not be expanded. Fortunately, one of the party on board was a shipbuilder, and he ordered all hands to the rear end of the craft. This shifting of weight lifted the bow clear of the mud, the cylinders slid outward, and the *Nautilus* broke free. Clearly unreliable, the boat did not receive official support and was given up.

Another abortive experiment in England was the steam-powered *Resurgam* (Latin for "I will rise again"), designed by a clergyman, George William Garret. Garret's idea was to build up a tremendous pressure in the boiler before submerging, which he calculated would give him enough steam for fifteen miles of subsurface cruising. There was no reserve air supply; Garret's figures told him that the air contained in the crew compartment would be ample for the planned period of submergence. However, the boat did not live up to its name. On a trial run it sank with its crew and failed to rise again. Nevertheless, Garret's ideas seem to have influenced a Swedish gunmaker named Thorsten Nordenfeldt, who became interested in submersibles. Garret may also have worked with Nordenfeldt on the design of his boats.

Nordenfeldt built several steam-driven submersibles between 1885 and 1888. He used a system of keeping a reserve supply of steam in insulated containers. Just before submerging, the fire was sealed off, and the boat proceeded on its reserve supply of steam. Nordenfeldt's submersibles were intended to do most of their cruising afloat or awash, submerging only briefly when they came close to the enemy.

Nordenfeldt I, the first of the series, was reportedly sold to the Greek government.

The second was sold to the Greeks' age-old enemy, Turkey. *Nordenfeldt II* performed spectacularly before the Sultan of Turkey, darting nimbly through the swift currents of the Bosporus and submerging and surfacing like a whale. However, at its official trials before the navy, the boat refused to submerge properly, and when it fired a torpedo, the bow popped up, the stern went down, and *Nordenfeldt II* was almost rammed by a passing ship. Despite the unsatisfactory performance, the Turkish government decided to buy the boat —but apparently hoped to avoid paying for it. Eventually the bill was settled, and the boat was left to rust at its dock in Constantinople (now Istanbul), for the Turkish sailors did not have the mechanical skill to manage it. The last Nordenfeldt boat, larger and more powerful than the others, was sold to Russia, despite a poor showing in its trials.

The steam-powered submarine Nordenfeldt II *lies at anchor. Men on its deck give an indication of its size.*

Spain came close to becoming a submarine power when a naval officer named Isaac Peral designed a highly maneuverable electric submarine. At this point in his career, Peral was teaching physics and chemistry at the Spanish naval academy, and electricity seems to have been his special field of interest. The submarine, named *Peral* after its inventor, was launched at Cadiz in 1887. Its cigar-shaped hull was seventy feet long and nine feet in diameter, and it was driven by twin thirty-horsepower electric motors, each turning its own propeller. (The total horsepower was roughly equivalent to that of twenty present-day gas-powered lawn-mowers. Peral's power was limited by the number of batteries he could pack into the hull.) Three small motors drove the air pumps and a pair of vertical propellers for depth control. A powerful electric search-light mounted on the underside of the hull provided illumination for examining the ocean floor, a feature found in modern re-search submersibles. Six hundred battery cells supplied the power for all these—there could not have been much room left over for the crew.

The *Peral* performed well in its trials, and the newspapers and the public heaped honors on the inventor. The papers carried telegraphed, on-the-spot reports of the trials. Streets were named for Peral, and the Queen of Spain presented him with a sword of honor. He was made a nobleman, with the rank of marquis, and given a na-tional award of half a million pesetas. Later, jealous rivals in the Spanish navy managed to circulate unfavorable official reports on the boat's performance, and the project was killed. The papers and the public now turned against Peral, and the former national hero fell into disgrace.

One of the best-remembered submers-ibles of the United States was the *Intelligent Whale,* built in New Jersey in 1872. Hand-propelled, its bulbous twenty-six-foot hull carried a crew of thirteen. The *Intelligent Whale* is significant for oceano-graphic submersibles only because it had a hatch through which a diver could pass while the vessel was submerged.

This was successfully demonstrated by a General Sweeney, who donned a diving suit, left the boat in sixteen feet of water, and blew up an old scow with a torpedo. On the strength of this, the United States government bought the *Intelligent Whale.* It was a very bad investment, for the un-wieldy craft sank and had to be fished up repeatedly. Thirty-nine men were drowned before it was retired from service.

Submersible construction during the last quarter of the nineteenth century was dominated by two remarkable men, John Philip Holland and Simon Lake.

Holland was born in Ireland in 1841. A frail, sickly child, he had hopes of a career at sea, but his eyes were too weak. As he wryly joked in later life, no one would trust him even to row a two-oared boat, much less navigate a ship. Instead, he joined the Order of Christian Brothers and became an elementary-school teacher, thus keeping up his studies in science and mathematics. At the age of thirty-two he left the Order (he had not yet taken his final vows) and came to the United States.

During his childhood, Holland had lived through the terrible suffering of the potato famine. Potatoes were then the main crop of Ireland and the main food of the Irish people. But in the 1840s the potato crop was destroyed for several years running by a mysterious blight, and people were left penniless and starving. Through a combination of callousness, fear, and bureaucratic bungling, the British government did very little to help the Irish. Hundreds of thousands of people died as a result. Although Holland himself did not suffer—his father was a coast guard officer and had a steady salary—the experience left him permanently embittered toward Britain. In the United States he became involved with the Fenian Brotherhood, a group of Irish revolutionaries who were attempting to free Ireland from British rule. To these men he proposed building a submarine torpedo boat to destroy British shipping. The Fenians collected funds and encouraged him to go ahead.

Holland had become interested in submarines while in his twenties, and he had planned one while still in Ireland. He had sent improved plans to the United States Navy in 1875, only to have them rejected as impractical. Now, backed by the Fenians, he was able to put his plans into practice.

He began experimenting with a small, one-man boat, which was completed in 1878. It was sixteen feet long, two and one half feet deep, and three feet wide, barely leaving room for the operator, who was dressed in a diving suit, to squeeze in. Actually, only a man as small and slight as Holland could have fitted into the space. The diving suit was necessary because the operator was supposed to leave the submarine to attach his torpedoes to the ships

John P. Holland peers confidently from the hatchway of one of his early submarines.

he intended to destroy. (Holland soon found this risky and impractical.)

The operator sat on the floor of the little submarine, legs stretched out in front of him, and navigated with the aid of a primitive periscope. This viewer gave such a poor image that Holland insisted for years afterward that the only proper way to navigate while submerged was by compass, rising now and then to take a sight on the enemy. Power came from a small internal-combustion engine of a peculiar type invented by a Boston engineer named George Brayton. Unfortunately, the engine refused to work; so Holland resourcefully ran a hose from the engine to the boiler of a small steam launch. Due to the peculiar construction of the engine, this worked. Holland was able to drive the tiny submersible forward and backward, dive, and rise—as long as he stayed close to the launch. His tests completed, he removed the machinery and scuttled the hull in the Passaic River.

The next boat was to be a full-fledged combat vessel, armed with explosive projectiles. It was designed to carry a crew of three: a navigator, an engineer, and a gunner to fire the projectiles from a pneumatic tube, a sort of air cannon. A redesigned Brayton engine, this time one that worked, drove the boat. For submerged operation, the engine was fed compressed air from the air tanks and vented its exhaust into the water.

While it was being built, agents from Sweden, Italy, Russia, Germany, and Turkey prowled the shipyard, diligently taking notes. After the launching, an inquisitive reporter kept after Holland, begging to be allowed to see the inside of the mystery vessel. Holland naturally refused. The reporter, desperate for a story, called upon his imagination and wrote up a colorful and highly inaccurate account of the "Fenian Ram" lurking in the Hudson River. The name stuck.

The *Fenian Ram,* launched in 1881, had a short career. A bitter quarrel broke out between factions of the Fenians, and one faction stole the *Fenian Ram,* along with a sixteen-foot scale model that Holland had built to test other theories of his. It was a melodramatic kidnapping. On a dark, cold November night, a little group of conspirators steered a tugboat up to the dock where the *Fenian Ram* was tied. They presented a forged note from Holland to the night watchman. They then deftly secured a towline to the bow of the

Ram, and also slid the smaller boat into the water, tying it to the stern of the *Ram.* Then they set off for New Haven, where a sympathizer had offered them mooring space. On the way, the model submarine, whose hatch had not been properly closed, sank in choppy water. Holland, knowing that the conspirators could not operate the *Fenian Ram,* vowed to let it rot on their hands. (Its only service to the cause of Irish independence came years later, in 1916, when it was shown at a bazaar to raise money.)

After the *Fenian Ram,* Holland had little success until 1893, when a group of lawyers and businessmen decided to invest in Holland and set up the Holland Torpedo Boat Company, hiring him as general manager at $50 a month. These backers had been attracted by the fact that Holland had won a United States Navy contract to build a submarine torpedo boat. Although the contract was killed by political intrigue, a new contract came through in 1895. Now the navy wanted Holland to build a large steam-and-electric-powered submersible, the *Plunger.* During construction, United States Navy experts, who knew nothing whatsoever about submarines, interfered repeatedly, making radical changes in Holland's designs. Holland realized that these changes would be disastrous; so on his own he started work on another submarine, the *Holland VI,* this one with a gasoline-electric power system. The *Plunger* failed, as Holland had predicted, and the *Holland VI,* launched early in 1898, performed admirably.

At that time tension was growing between the United States and Spain over Spain's possession of Cuba. Theodore

Boatyard of the Holland Torpedo Boat Company. The submarine next to the tugboat is the troublesome Plunger.

Roosevelt, then assistant secretary of the navy, urged the government in vain to buy *Holland VI*. When the Spanish-American War broke out, Holland offered personally to destroy the Spanish fleet in Santiago harbor if the government would transport his submarine there. The offer was turned down. Not until 1900 did the government concede its error and buy the submarine. Holland, meanwhile, was broke, and his backers agreed to sell the Holland Torpedo Boat Company to the newly formed Electric Boat Company. (This company eventually became the largest submarine builder in the United States; in 1955 it completed the world's first atomic-powered submarine, the famous *Nautilus,* named for Verne's fictional submarine.)

Unfortunately, Holland's backers were unscrupulous. They managed to get most of his patents assigned to the company, in which they held the controlling shares,

rather than to Holland. Thus, all royalties went to the company instead of to Holland, who himself owned only a small share of the stock. Up to 1900 they never paid him more than $90 a week, and in 1904 they maneuvered him out of the company entirely. This treatment by his associates was a source of great bitterness to Holland in his last years. Nevertheless, before his death in 1914 he saw his design adopted as the standard one for submarines in the world's navies.

Submarine inventors from Fulton on down had assured the world that their boats would bring world peace by making naval wars so destructive that no nation would risk one. And so they did their best to make their boats as lethal as possible. Simon Lake was one of the few who actually preferred to design submersibles for peaceful uses.

Simon Lake was born in Pleasantville,

New Jersey, in 1866. As a boy, he read Jules Verne's *Twenty Thousand Leagues under the Sea* and was forever after fascinated with the idea of underwater travel and exploration. In fact, though only ten or eleven years old, he immediately tried to improve on the design of the fictional *Nautilus*.

Lake had a stormy childhood. Brought up by an extremely strict stepgrandmother, he was always getting into fights at school and getting himself into trouble with the teachers. He found relief in working with tools and machinery, and eventually developed into a talented mechanical inventor.

As a young man Lake invented a safety steering device for bicycles and a noiseless winch for oyster dredges. He went into business manufacturing them in Balti-

more, but his mind was still full of plans for an underwater boat. In 1893 he was one of the competitors for the government contract that John Holland won. Meanwhile, Lake did not give up. He began calling on New York businessmen with his design for an underwater salvage boat. One after another, they enthusiastically ushered the red-haired young inventor out of their offices. And so, in 1894, he built a crude, home-made prototype to demonstrate the workability of his ideas. He named it *Argonaut Jr.*

Argonaut Jr. was hardly a craft to inspire confidence. Because Lake was almost broke, he built it as cheaply as possible. For the hull, he used two layers of pitch pine—a cheap, low-grade wood—with a waterproof layer of canvas sandwiched in between. For extra water-

Simon Lake, in middle-age here, poses in the deteriorated remains of Argonaut Jr., *his first submersible.*

Painters at work on Argonaut I. *The submersible's huge iron wheels are ridged for a better grip on the bottom.*

proofing he painted the outside with tar. The compressed-air tank was a salvaged carbon-dioxide cylinder bought from the owner of a bankrupt soda fountain. The entire craft was only fourteen feet long, five feet high, and four and one half feet across the beam. It looked like a flatiron on wheels, for it had two large wooden wheels in front for crawling along the bottom, powered by a hand crank and a bicycle chain. There was a smaller rear wheel for steering.

Lake had built in an air lock which would allow him to leave the submarine, explore the bottom, and return to the shelter of the boat. He cobbled together a diving helmet which he had fashioned out of sheet iron, with a tunic of painted canvas. To hold him down on the bottom, he tied window-sash weights to his legs. The ridiculous combination worked well enough for Lake's purpose, which was simply to conduct demonstrations in shallow water.

Exhibiting *Argonaut Jr.* in New York, the peppery, redheaded young man revealed a flair for publicity, and he easily captured the attention of the press and the public. Contributions from the public enabled him to get under way with the construction of the next *Argonaut,* one of a series designed for salvage use. Launched in 1897, this craft, *Argonaut I,* was a sizable boat, thirty-six feet long, with seven-foot cast-iron wheels for traveling on the bottom. It was powered by a thirty-horse-power gasoline engine that breathed through a snorkel tube supported by a float. This, of course, limited the depth to which it could dive. As a safety device, Lake provided a heavy, detachable keel. By dropping the keel, the submarine could float to the surface.

Lake worked on the theory that a submarine should be slightly heavier than the water, flying through the water with the aid of its hydroplanes (his name for diving planes). Holland, in contrast, held that a submarine should have a slight positive buoyancy so that if anything went wrong it would automatically float to the surface.

Ironically, *Argonaut I* was built at the same Baltimore shipyard where Holland's *Plunger* was being constructed. The two men worked in adjoining rooms for months without saying so much as hello to each other.

To gain publicity, Lake staged an underwater party for the press aboard *Argonaut I*. Twenty journalists were invited, including one celebrated female reporter. More guests showed up than had been expected, but one or two suddenly felt ill when it was time to board the submarine, one announced that he had a weak heart and could not stand excitement, and one remembered that his life insurance policy had lapsed; so there was room for all who wanted to go. The submergence went smoothly, and Lake and his guests drank a toast in champagne at the bottom of Chesapeake Bay. Later, the guests were allowed to rake up shells from the bottom through the air lock.

When the Spanish-American War broke out, Lake, like Holland, offered his submarine to the government and was also turned down. After annoying the navy by performing maneuvers around the big naval base at Hampton Roads, Virginia, Lake took *Argonaut I* on a voyage of about a thousand miles down Chesapeake Bay and up the Atlantic coast to New York. Most of this voyage took place on the surface, but several hundred miles

were traveled underwater. Not only was this the longest underwater voyage accomplished up to that time; it was also the first extended oceanographic observation of the sea bottom.

In the same year, Lake took a Kodak camera down and took snapshots of the fish peering in through the windows of his submarine. These were among the first underwater photographs ever made.

Unusual and even bizarre designs abounded in the late nineteenth century. Men in several countries, including the United States, invented and even built submarines with screwlike hulls, designed to spin through the water with the steadiness of a rifle bullet. A nonmoving compartment was to hold passengers and crew. All were failures.

A Californian named Gerber devised a submersible to be powered by rubber bands. He proposed to use it to search for the chariot wheels of Pharaoh's army at the bottom of the Red Sea.

A Brooklyn inventor named Alvarez-Templo designed an "aquapede," or underwater bicycle. It was to be a sixteen-foot aluminum cylinder with a well in the middle for the operator, who wore a diving suit and helmet and pedaled vigorously to turn the propeller. There was also a handlebar that carried controls for the rudder and diving planes. An electric headlamp on the nose of the "aquapede" lighted the diver's way. Although the main result of this invention was to provide newspaper cartoonists with a subject, it can be considered a forerunner of the diving sled used by Cousteau and his teams in their underwater explorations.

A more practical invention was the salvage submersible built in 1897 by an Italian nobleman, Count Piatti dal Pozzo. Built in France, it was named the *Travailleur Sous-marin* (*Underwater Worker*) or *La France*. It was a steel sphere ten feet in diameter, with walls nearly two inches thick, which the count calculated would give it a safe working depth of more than 330 feet. It was designed to be hung by a cable from a surface ship, but it had three electrically powered propellers to position it over the worksite. A large, fixed rudder kept it from revolving around its suspension cable.

An electric power line and a telephone line linked the *Underwater Worker* to its surface support ship. For its work, it had a long arm on the bottom, fitted with a mechanical grab, which could be moved back and forth from inside the sphere. Around its waist the craft had a number of pivoted ballast buckets. In an emergency, the buckets could be dumped, and the sphere, being slightly lighter than water, would float to the surface. A French writer compared it aptly to an underwater captive balloon.

Although the *Underwater Worker* was not put to actual use, it worked successfully in tests, and it can be considered a forerunner of William Beebe's famous bathysphere of the 1930s.

7

The Submarine Arrives

THE early years of the twentieth century saw nations engaged in a frantic race to build up their submarine flotillas. Although no submersible had sunk a ship in combat since the disastrous success of the *David* in the Civil War, the lesson was clear. A concealed submarine with self-propelled torpedoes could, without warning, sink a far more powerful surface ship. Even the mightiest battleship was helpless against this surprise attack, which submarines were now well able to deliver. It was becoming plain to naval strategists that a weak nation with a small fleet of submarines could deliver a knockout blow to a powerful surface navy.

France, Britain, Russia, Germany, Italy, Sweden, Chile, Argentina, the United States, Austria-Hungary, Norway, the Netherlands, Spain, Portugal, Brazil, and Japan all possessed submarines. Even little Denmark, with no building program of its own, had purchased a small electric-powered submarine from an Italian shipyard. John Holland's designs were being used by at least four countries.

In 1900 the United States Navy had bought *Holland VI,* following up with a contract for six more submarines. In the fall of 1900, *Holland VI* "destroyed" a battleship in war games, and the commander of the sub reported that he could probably have destroyed three ships without being discovered. The following year, the first of the new series of Holland submarines, the *Fulton,* set a record by spending fifteen hours on the sea floor, using only the air supply contained in its tanks. Most experts had not believed such a long submergence possible without some provision for getting air from the surface.

In 1900 Britain, too, began building a series of Holland boats, using plans sold to them by the Electric Boat Company. It

Holland's record-breaking Fulton *lies beside its sister submarine* Porpoise *in this 1902 photograph.*

Britain's first submarine—designed by John Holland—dangles from a mighty shipyard crane (1901).

must have galled the old Fenian sympathizer to see the British government using the boats he had originally invented in order to destroy their sea power, but he had no control over the company that owned his patents.

A peculiar series of disasters struck the British series of boats, known as the A-boats, and some people accused Holland of deliberately altering the plans to make the boats sink. However, Holland was known as an honorable man, and it is unlikely that he would have taken such dastardly revenge. It is much more likely that the accidents were the result of "improvements" made in Holland's plans by other persons at the Electric Boat Company, over whom he had no authority. Holland often had to suffer the humiliation of seeing his plans changed by inexperienced young naval architects who pointed out that they, after all, held engineering degrees from Annapolis, while Holland was merely an untrained schoolteacher.

In the Far East, Japan and Russia confronted each other on increasingly bad terms. Each country had plans to take over northeastern China and Korea. The Japanese, far outnumbered by their Russian rivals, were very interested in weapons that could help them overcome Russia's numerical superiority.

Even as early as 1897, Japanese naval experts had inspected *Holland VI* and taken dives in it. When the Russo-Japanese War broke out early in 1904, Japan ordered five of the A-class submarines from the Electric Boat Company. It also bought from Holland himself (now out of the company) the plans for two new-type submarines, larger, faster, and with a much longer cruising range. Before the submarines had been completed, the Japanese Navy had annihilated the Russian fleet at the battle of Tsushima Strait; so they had no trial in combat. Japan nevertheless went on to develop a fleet of fast, long-range Holland-type submarines.

Russia, too, bought a number of Holland submarines.

Japan had also approached Simon Lake. Russian spies learned about this, and Russia made Lake a very generous offer in order to keep his submarines out of the hands of the Japanese. One submarine was ready for delivery—the *Protector*—but by then war had broken out, and the neutrality laws of the United States forbade Lake to sell weapons to either belligerent. So the *Protector,* minus its batteries so that Lake could claim it was "incomplete," was towed to a secret rendezvous with a Russian freighter. (The Holland subs, for the same reason, had been disassembled and sneaked past the customs officials as "parts.") Before dawn on a rainy, densely foggy Sunday morning, the submarine was swung up on the Russian ship's deck, hidden under tarpaulins, and smuggled out of the country.

Lake followed soon afterward, entering Russia on a false passport supplied by the Russian government. He stayed long enough to build five more *Protectors* and six larger cruising submarines. Leaving Russia, he was offered a contract by the great arms-manufacturing firm of Krupp, which was then making submarines for both Germany and Russia. The contract fell through, but meanwhile the Germans had had time to copy Lake's designs, and to the end of his career he insisted that the deadly U-boats of World War I were based on his ideas.

Submarines were still a long way from perfection, and they were distressingly subject to accidents. There were a number of cases of crews being poisoned by carbon monoxide leaking from the exhaust pipes of the gasoline engines. In some cases, gasoline fumes felled the crew. There were fires and explosions caused by care-

The Protector, *first of a series of military submarines designed by Simon Lake.*

A cross-sectional diagram of a Protector-*class submarine. Faint outlines show wheels lowered for bottom travel.*

less sailors smoking near spilled gasoline, or by sparks from the electrical equipment. Even the batteries could be deadly. During recharging, they gave off quantities of hydrogen gas, which is highly explosive. It is also invisible, odorless, and tasteless. Now and then something caused a spark near the undetected cloud of hydrogen around the batteries, and a violent explosion followed.

The gasoline engine was gradually eliminated as diesel power was developed. The fuel that a diesel engine burns is heavier and less volatile than gasoline, which greatly reduces the danger caused by fumes. To ignite its fuel, the diesel engine uses the same principle that makes a tire pump heat up: compressing a gas raises its temperature. Air in the cylinder of a diesel engine is compressed to about one-sixteenth of its original volume. This raises it to red-hot temperature. When the fuel is sprayed into the cylinder, the hot air ignites it immediately. Therefore a diesel engine needs no complicated, trouble-prone electrical system of gener-

ator, coils, distributor, spark plugs, and wiring. In addition, a diesel engine gets much more mileage out of each drop of fuel than a gasoline engine of equal horsepower.

Along with these advantages, diesel engines had some big drawbacks. They were much bulkier and heavier than gasoline engines, horsepower for horsepower, and they shook and pounded dreadfully. In addition, they were considerably more expensive to build than gasoline engines. Nevertheless, submarine designers were thinking seriously about them as early as 1900, and France was using them in submarines as early as 1905. Germany and England soon followed suit. The last gasoline-powered submarines were not phased out, however, until after World War I.

Even while the race to build submarines was going on, many high-ranking naval officials remained quite doubtful about the value of the submarine. In Britain, especially, some officials were downright scornful. Simon Lake had heard his submarines pooh-poohed by a British naval expert who said, "We know all about submarines. They are weapons of the weaker power. They are very poor fighting machines and can be of no possible use to the mistress of the seas [Britain]."

Another British admiral remarked that the great value of building submarines was to teach navy officers and sailors their weaknesses when used against them.

In the early 1900s, the admirals still had some basis for their contemptuous attitudes. But in less than fifteen years, submarines improved rapidly.

World War I broke out in the first week of August 1914. On August 12 John Holland died, disappointed and embittered by the treatment he had received from his country and his business associates. On September 22, forty days after Holland's death, a single German U-boat sank three

British cruisers in one hour and five minutes, sending fourteen hundred men to their deaths. The submarine had arrived.

During the first year of the war, U-boats (the name comes from *Unterseeboot,* the German for "undersea boat") sank nearly three hundred ships belonging to Britain and other nations. But the resourceful British devised antisubmarine countermeasures, including the hydrophone, an underwater listening apparatus that could pick up the noise of a submerged U-boat's electric motors and propellers. When a submarine was heard, depth charges were dropped, in the hope of crushing the submarine's hull by the force of the underwater explosion. The submarine's best chance for escape was to sink to the bottom and cut its motors, hiding in silence. Some submarines, on both sides, took refuge at depths beyond their known limits, re-

A U-boat halts a merchant steamer. Such pictures are rare, as news photographers were seldom on hand.

turned safely, and thus much was learned about the stresses a submarine could endure. But the developments of the period up to the end of World War I were not limited to the military field.

A working submersible intended for sponge fishing was designed by a French priest in the city of Tunis. Named *Bou-Korn* for a famous nearby mountain, its sixteen-foot, lemon-shaped hull had three propellers for forward and sidewise maneuvering, and mechanical arms. It was unusual in having a metal hull sheathed in wood. Though accidentally sunk at its dock, it was salvaged and used successfully for many years.

In retirement John Holland had also turned his mind to peaceful uses for submersibles. He designed a forty-passenger submarine for amusement rides at seaside resorts. The sides of the vessel were to be lined with large viewports to give the customers a good look at the undersea panorama. The inventor calculated that at current prices the operators of such an underwater pleasure craft could count on making $200 a day—twenty weeks' wages in many occupations at that time. He also designed a passenger submarine for crossing the English Channel, a body of water that is notorious for making passengers seasick because of its roughness. A submarine, of course, could travel beneath the turbulent surface zone, sparing its passengers several hours of discomfort and nausea. Neither boat was ever built, however. Holland also prophesied the role of the submarine in scientific research, but many years were to pass before his predictions came true.

Simon Lake never gave up his boyhood dreams of using underwater boats for salvage and exploration. In the late 1890s he had done some profitable salvage work in Long Island Sound with *Argonaut II* (this was *Argonaut I* rebuilt as a larger vessel). He had recovered valuable cargoes of copper ore and coal, and he had invented submersible cargo carriers. These were tanklike containers into which the cargo could be loaded at the bottom. When full, the cargo carriers would have air pumped into their ballast tanks to float them to the surface. They were then towed into harbor by an ordinary tugboat.

Lake also invented an unusual salvage device that combined a bottom-crawling submersible with a long, wide tube reaching to the surface. A diver was to slide down the tube to the submersible, maneuver it to his worksite, and emerge through an air lock to do his job. He returned to the surface by way of the same tube, which was rigged to a support ship that supplied compressed air and electric power to the submersible.

He actually built a version of this apparatus, a ninety-five-foot-long tube with an air lock at the bottom, with which he intended to salvage the treasure of the *Lutine,* a French warship that had gone down off the Dutch coast in the 1790s, loaded with money. Dutch fishermen occasionally pulled up gold coins from the *Lutine* in their nets, not enough to make them rich, but enough to encourage a series of unsuccessful treasure hunters. Lake never carried out this project, because Congress suddenly indicated an interest in purchasing his submarines for the navy, and he returned to the United States. Later, he became very interested in salvaging the purser's safe from the *Lusitania,* an unarmed British passenger ship that was sunk without warning by a German submarine in 1915. Nothing came of this project, either.

However, Germany built two cargo-carrying submarines, the world's first and, so far, also the last. One, the *Deutschland,* made two successful voyages from Germany to Baltimore, where there was a large and sympathetic German-American population. The other, the *Bremen,* was lost at sea on its first voyage and never reached America.

The *Deutschland*'s arrival caused tremendous excitement. Never before had such a voyage been attempted. Simon Lake's dream, the cargo-carrying submersible, was at last a reality. Lake himself hurried down to Baltimore, though not to congratulate the German captain. His intention was to seize the *Deutschland* for infringement of his patents. The German consul at Baltimore, however, cleverly ap-

The German cargo submarine Deutschland *being towed up Chesapeake Bay.*

pealed to Lake's vanity, admitting that the *Deutschland* really was based on his designs and predicting a great future for cargo-carrying submersibles, if only the *Deutschland* were allowed to demonstrate their advantages. "Would you strangle your own baby?" the consul asked Lake.

The wily consul also played on Lake's resentment of the British blockade of Germany, which interfered with America's freedom of trade (America was still neutral), and hinted at big contracts from the German government after England had been put in her place. Lake relented and called off his lawsuit.

Remarkable as the *Deutschland*'s voyage was, its significance should not be overrated. For one thing, the total cargo capacity of the *Deutschland* was only six hundred tons, far less than that of the average freight steamer. This was not because torpedoes took up most of the space, for the *Deutschland* was unarmed. It was simply that a submarine's cargo space is naturally limited. Another point that is often overlooked is that practically all of the *Deutschland*'s voyage was made on the surface. The captain told Lake that he had sailed only eighty miles under water, out of a total of about four thousand miles. Wishing to make his best speed and spare his batteries and crew, he had stuck to the surface, submerging only to escape detection by ships, and to avoid one bad storm.

Germany turned to a submarine cargo-carrier only because her surface freighters could not slip through the British blockade. The voyage was profitable only because the *Deutschland* carried very valuable cargoes that both countries needed badly: scarce synthetic dyes for the

United States, which at that time could not make them; and rubber and nickel for Germany, whose war machine needed these strategic materials desperately. Today, as then, cargo-carrying submersibles can pay their way only under a special set of conditions.

World War I did more than establish the submarine as a serious military weapon. It did a great deal to advance the design and construction of submarines and underwater equipment. Underwater sound-location techniques took a dramatic leap forward under the pressure of wartime needs, as did escape techniques for the crews of damaged subs. Gyroscopic devices were used to guide torpedoes automatically, and gyrocompasses kept submarines on course. More powerful engines and batteries were made, and submarines became faster and farther-ranging. Not least important, naval men were becoming familiar with them and learning how to handle them. All this would bear fruit

later in the development of oceanographic submersibles.

The United States had entered the war far behind other nations in submarine development. Its subs were small, obsolete, poorly designed, and usually poorly built. Some were barely seaworthy. The quality of American submarines remained poor after the war. In one shocking case, several holes were discovered in the hull plates of a submarine under construction. Although small, they could cause fatal leaks when the boat submerged. When the defect was pointed out to the foreman, he replied sullenly that the holes would not show when the paint job was finished!

Even when shipyard workers were conscientious, poorly trained crewmen caused costly accidents. One submarine sank at its dock when a crewman, filling the batteries with water, knocked off work and forgot to turn his hose off. The submarine filled with water, lost its buoyancy, and went to the bottom. (A similar accident happened

The U.S. submarine S-1, like a number of subs built in the 1920s, was large enough to carry its own spotter plane.

to a nuclear submarine around 1970.) Another sank beside its tender vessel because a crewman had taken out a sea valve for repairs and forgotten to replace it. A third submarine sank on its trial run with several navy officers and over thirty workers from the shipyard where it was built. The reason: someone had neglected to install a manhole cover in the stern ballast tank. Fortunately, the water was only sixty feet deep, and the bow of the sub was still slightly buoyant, so all the occupants were able to crawl to safety through a torpedo tube.

Batteries continued to explode while being recharged, and submarines continued to collide with other vessels. In one bizarre incident, the nearly new submarine *S-4* was run over and sunk by a Coast Guard patrol ship searching for rumrunners. The crew perished because violent storms held up the rescue work.

These tragedies and near-tragedies forced the navy to devise new equipment for rescuing the trapped crews and new techniques for using it. One useful one was the Momsen "lung," a self-contained breathing apparatus with which a man could swim to the surface from his sunken submarine. The lung was originally invented in England around 1905 by a man named Davis. It was complicated and not too satisfactory in practice. No lungs or other escape equipment were installed on American submarines until after the disaster of the *S-4,* which took place in December 1927.

Some earlier submarine accidents had roused little public concern, but the attempts to rescue *S-4* had been covered in detail by the nation's press. The sense of tragedy was heightened by the fact that some of the trapped crew survived for three days, banging out messages to rescue divers with a hammer on their steel hull. The resulting public indignation forced the navy to take action. A lieutenant named Charles B. Momsen worked out a simplified version of the old Davis lung. To prove that it worked, he made demonstration "escapes" from submarines at depths of over 120 feet. Soon it was adopted as standard equipment. Other navies also adopted similar devices.

Essentially, the Momsen lung resembled a gas mask with a bag into which the wearer breathed. Before putting the mask on, an escaping submariner would fill the bag with oxygen from a cylinder on the submarine. Once in the water, he breathed the same air over and over. A chemical filter removed the carbon dioxide from the air so that he could breathe it safely. (Too much carbon dioxide causes unconsciousness and eventually death.) To avoid the bends, he was trained to stop every ten feet, guided by indicators on a line supported by a buoy.

At first, some crewmen suffered mysterious collapses during their training. Two even died, one of them in only sixteen feet of water. A long series of experiments found the answer. The men had held their breath as they ascended. As they rose, the pressure of the water on their chests became less and less, while the pressure of the air inside their lungs remained as high as when they had breathed it in. The result was that the air expanded, rupturing the lungs. It takes no more than a rise of six feet for this to happen. When this had been learned, submariners were trained to breathe evenly as they ascended, and there were no more such accidents.

Valuable as the Momsen lung was in escapes, it could not protect men from the cold and pressure of the depths. To counter these dangers, various types of rescue chambers, which worked on the principle of the diving bell, were invented.

Although improved safety procedures had cut the rate of submarine accidents to a very low level, the rescue chamber proved its value in the spring of 1939, when the new U.S. submarine *Squalus,* on a test dive off the coast of New Hampshire, flooded and sank. Twenty-six men lost their lives in the flooded after-section of the boat, but thirty-three survived in the bow section. At that time all new submarines were built with escape locks, and there were Momsen lungs for every crew member. But the *Squalus* lay 243 feet down, far deeper than a Momsen lung had ever been used, and the water was at freezing temperature. The commander of the *Squalus,* Lieutenant Oliver Naquin, did not wish to expose his men to such risks except as a last resort, for he knew that the ice-cold water could freeze an unprotected man to death in a few minutes.

Since the *Squalus* had sunk near the big naval base at Portsmouth, New Hampshire, Naquin knew that rescuers could not be far away. He sent up an emergency buoy with a telephone inside, one of the pieces of rescue equipment the navy had developed after the disaster of the *S-4.* As he hoped, the buoy was soon spotted by a search vessel, the *Squalus's* sister submarine *Sculpin.* However, before the two commanders had a chance to exchange information, a big wave snapped the buoy's lines. But the *Sculpin* radioed a message for help, and the rescue ship *Falcon* rushed to the area. On its deck was a rescue bell designed by Commander Allan McCann of the United States Navy, which had never been used.

Once on the scene, a diver from the *Falcon* went down to the *Squalus* and quickly fastened a stout wire cable to the escape-hatch cover of the submarine. The rescue bell was lowered over the side of the *Falcon* and wound itself down this guide line by a compressed-air motor. When it met the *Squalus's* hull, the operators of the bell carefully maneuvered it until its opening fitted over the hatch of the *Squalus.* The bell's lower portion was blown clear of water, then air pressure was reduced. The pressure of the sea forced the bell down tightly against the submarine's hull, and a thick rubber gasket around the mouth of the bell made a leakproof seal.

The hatch was opened, and the first load of survivors, chilled to the bone and groggy from breathing used air, were helped into the bell. The hatch was closed, the vacuum seal broken, and the bell wound itself back to the surface. Three trips were made, until the last survivors were safe aboard the *Falcon.* The McCann bell had set a new depth record for underwater rescues. A rescue at 243 feet was proof that mastery of the underwater world was becoming a reality.

Remarkable progress had been made in the design of a diving chamber for purely scientific use. William Beebe, a zoologist, had become fascinated by undersea life during expeditions to Bermuda, where he had made a number of shallow dives to explore the coral reefs. From this start, he

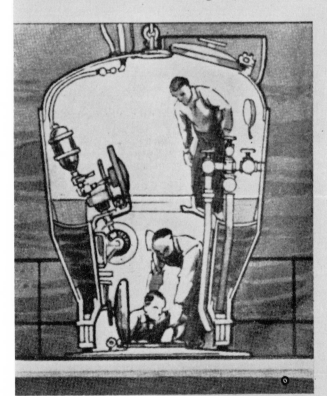

Chamber being hoisted overboard
for a test submergence

Rescued man being assisted through
hatch to the upper compartment of chamber

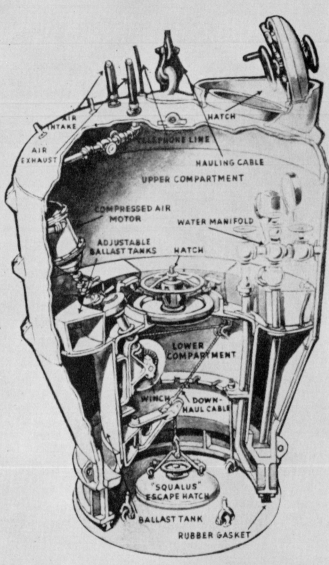

RESCUE CHAMBER USED ON
U.S. SUBMARINE *SQUALUS*

AIR
INTAKE

AIR
EXHAUST

TELEPHONE LINE

HATCH

HAULING CABLE

UPPER COMPARTMENT

COMPRESSED AIR
MOTOR

WATER MANIFOLD

ADJUSTABLE
BALLAST TANKS

HATCH

LOWER
COMPARTMENT

WINCH

DOWN-
HAUL CABLE

"SQUALUS"
ESCAPE HATCH

BALLAST TANK

RUBBER GASKET

Vertical section of rescue chamber.
The lower compartment and the enveloping
ballast tank are alternately flooded and
drained at different stages of operation.
Normally when one of these spaces is flooded
the other is empty, but exceptional conditions may alter this procedure. An air-line
for blowing the water from these spaces is
not shown here

This rescue bell was used to save the crew of the Squalus, *trapped in a crippled submarine under
243 feet of water.*

wanted to go on to make first-hand observations of the deep-sea creatures he had only seen mangled and dying in his nets. To do this, he would need to go hundreds of feet beyond the depth a diving suit would allow. Only a rigid chamber could protect him from the terrific pressure.

In the late 1920s he began designing cylindrical diving chambers, but soon realized that their flat ends would cause them to be crushed too easily. His thoughts turned to a sphere instead. Because it resists pressure equally in all directions, a sphere can stand a great deal more pressure than any other shape. In fact, within the limits of its material, a sphere actually becomes stronger as the water presses in on it from all around. Beebe was a naturalist, not a marine engineer, and so he joined forces with a wealthy engineer named Otis Barton, who took care of the actual design

and construction of the spherical diving chamber.

In 1930 the sphere, remodeled several times, was ready. Beebe named it *Bathysphere,* from the Greek *bathys* (deep) plus sphere, for its shape. The bathysphere was built of $1\frac{1}{4}$-inch-thick steel and weighed 5400 pounds—over $2\frac{1}{2}$ tons. Only 4 feet 9 inches in outside diameter, it left little room for observers inside, but making it bigger would have meant increasing its weight. Extra weight was dangerous because the bathysphere had no reserve buoyancy. It was held up only by a single steel cable, 7/8 inch thick. If the cable snapped, the bathysphere would plummet to the bottom, with no hope of rescue for its occupants.

In addition to the support cable, there was a rubber cable that contained electric power and telephone lines from the sup-

William Beebe about to jump to deck after inspecting the Bathysphere. *Entrance to sphere is at left of picture.*

port vessel. The air supply of the bathysphere came from two small tanks of compressed oxygen, while trays of chemicals absorbed the carbon dioxide and water vapor the men breathed out. Two viewports of thick, ultrastrong quartz glass permitted the men to observe undersea phenomena, and there was a powerful electric searchlight for the depths beyond which natural light could not penetrate. The only entrance into the bathysphere was through a manhole fourteen inches wide. Fortunately, both Beebe and Barton were very slender.

After sending the empty bathysphere down for several test submergences, the men made their first real dive, to 800 feet. Beebe made valuable observations on the behavior of the light as the depth of the water increased. The surface layers were a sunny green (it was a sunny day), but at 50 feet the water became blue green. At 300 feet it was pale blue, and at 700 feet a very dark blue. (This gradual color change holds true only in very clear water.) At 800 feet the water was nearly black.

At 300 feet the two men had a bad scare: water was leaking in slowly around the door. On a hunch, Beebe phoned an order to the winchman on their support barge to lower them rapidly. As he had hoped, the increased pressure pushed the door cover tighter over the opening, and the leak did not increase. By coating the joint between the door and the manhole with white lead paste, they eliminated the leak on their later dives.

Beebe and Barton made several more dives that season. On the deepest, they reached 1,426 feet. Continuing his experi-

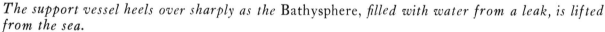

The support vessel heels over sharply as the Bathysphere, *filled with water from a leak, is lifted from the sea.*

ments with light and color effects, Beebe had brought along a bright red shrimp and a book with colored illustrations of sea animals. At 50 feet he noticed that the shrimp had turned from red to velvety black. He turned to a colored illustration of red shrimps. It, too, was black. All the red light had been absorbed by the water. As the sphere sank, he noticed the great abundance of life in the deeper layers of the water, which surprised him because his nets usually brought up very few organisms. Watching the agility of the fish and other organisms that swam and darted past his viewport, he realized that most of them could easily dodge the nets of scientists and fishermen. Lacking proper means of observation, scientists had formed completely incorrect ideas about life in the depths.

In the following years, Beebe and Barton made many more dives off the Bermuda coast in the bathysphere. Barton watched the instruments and took photographs through the viewports, while Beebe phoned descriptions of the creatures they saw up to an assistant on deck, who put them into writing. There were strange fish with luminous patterns on their bodies, glowing in blue, red, green, yellow, and purple. There were shrimp that shot out clouds of luminescent fluid, and tiny, monstrous-looking predators with huge mouths and daggerlike teeth, which could swallow fish larger than themselves. Many of these animals had never been seen before.

On one dive, Beebe made a radio broadcast as he descended from 1,500 to 2,200 feet, telephoning his commentary up to a radio transmitter on deck. On their deepest dive, in 1934, they reached 3,028 feet. With only a dozen turns of cable remaining on the winch, the captain of the support vessel refused to let out any more. With some anxiety as to whether the cable would hold, the bathynauts were reeled back in. Their depth record was unbeaten for fourteen years.

Their dives were not without frightening moments. Once, the telephone cable went bad, and they could not communicate with the surface crew. Another time the men installed a third quartz-glass viewpane and sent the bathysphere down to test its tightness. When the sphere was hauled back up, it was unusually heavy, and Beebe noticed a needlelike spray of water shooting out from the edge of the window. Realizing that the sphere had leaked and filled with high-pressure water, he ordered everyone out of the way and began to unscrew the big central bolt of the door. As he did so, a fine mist of water vapor spewed out. A few more turns, and the massive bolt tore loose and shot across the deck like a cannon shell, followed by a solid cylinder of water powerful enough to decapitate anyone standing in its way. The leaky pane was quickly replaced with the old steel plate.

Once heavy seas blew up while they were nearly two thousand feet down. Each time the support vessel rolled, the motion was transmitted along the cable with a whiplash effect, making things very uncomfortable for the men in the steel ball. That time, Beebe and Barton were in no real danger, but they almost lost their lives while contour diving along a coral reef. In contour diving, the bathysphere was towed slowly along, close to the bottom, while Beebe phoned instructions to the deck crew to raise or lower it as the bottom rose or fell. On one such dive, Beebe suddenly noticed a fifty-foot coral crag directly ahead, and not very far away. He gave an emergency order to raise the sphere as fast as possible, and they missed the crag by inches. Had the winchman delayed even a few seconds Beebe and Barton would have struck the massive rock, and the bathysphere might have been ripped loose. Although the contour dives were indeed dangerous, they revealed a great deal about the geology of Bermuda and the biology of a coral-reef community.

While Beebe was adding to man's knowledge of the life of the deep waters, an Arctic explorer, Sir Hubert Wilkins, attempted to reach the North Pole by submarine, planning to cruise trouble-free beneath the ice that blocked the way for surface ships. He bought an old World War I submarine, slated for scrapping, from the United States Navy, and renamed it *Nautilus*. He called upon Simon Lake, the original builder of the sub, to remodel it for polar conditions. Lake added a number of his inventions, including a retractable drill for boring through the surface ice in case the submarine could not find an open spot to come up for air and recharging batteries. The drill, a hollow tube, was wide enough for a man to climb through to the surface to take observations of weather conditions.

In 1931 the *Nautilus* began its voyage northward. Unfortunately, it was plagued by mechanical problems and frequent breakdowns. (Lake later said that it was because Wilkins, impatient to get started, left before the machinery could be properly overhauled.) The forward diving planes were carried away in an Arctic ice jam, so that one very shallow dive beneath the ice was all that Wilkins dared attempt. The *Nautilus* had to turn back 500 miles from the North Pole.

Nevertheless, the expedition was not a complete failure, because scientists aboard the submarine had secured some worthwhile samples of sea organisms, had taken soundings and charted some hitherto unknown sections of ocean bottom, and had removed core samples from the ocean floor. They also made the first gravity readings in the Arctic, and their findings were of interest to geologists. A third of a century later, similar findings made by submersibles would throw light on many questions about the sea.

8

Developments in Diving Gear

WHILE advances were being made in submersible design, equally important ones were also taking place with diving gear. In the early 1770s a Frenchman named Fréminet invented one of the earliest diving suits, with a simple, rigid helmet attached to a leather suit. A jointed metal framework supported the suit and kept the water from pressing on the diver's body, just as the rigid helmet protected his head. To get his air, the diver worked a bellows attached to a snorkel tube. Since the framework of the suit counteracted the water pressure, this system actually worked. In one test, a diver went down to fifty feet and stayed there for an hour. In 1776, with an improved version of his outfit, Fréminet himself made dives in the harbor of Brest, where he performed such practical demonstrations as raising a lost anchor from the harbor floor and nailing lead sheathing to the bottom of a boat. Fréminet called his invention a "hydrostatergatic machine," a bad try at making up a Greek word for performing work underwater. Although Fréminet had demonstrated the practical value of his suit, it never came into wide use.

In 1797 or 1798, a German named Kleingert invented another type of rigid diving suit. Basically, it was a metal cylinder that enclosed the diver's head and his body down to the hips. Airtight and watertight leather sleeves and trousers were attached to the metal cylinder to prevent leakage while giving the diver freedom of motion. The diver's air came, as in Fréminet's suit, from a breathing tube extending to the surface. Actually, it was a double tube, one tube for breathing in and one for breathing out. The diver inhaled through an ivory mouthpiece and exhaled through his nose into the cylinder. Each time he inhaled, the expansion of his chest would

In this highly imaginative scene, divers equipped with Fréminet suits perform a variety of salvage tasks, while at far right one rescues victims of a shipwreck.

force stale air out of his metal shell by way of the exhaust tube.

Kleingert tested this outfit in the Oder River at his home city of Breslau (now Wroclaw, Poland). It was hailed as a wonderful device for saving people who were drowning close to shore. A rescuer could simply don one of these suits and wade out into water many feet over his head, even if he did not know how to swim himself. (There is no record that it was ever used for lifesaving, however.) Apparently Kleingert's apparatus was fairly widely used for salvage operations. Although divers complained that it was uncomfortable, it probably let them move their arms and legs more freely than Fréminet's jointed metal framework did.

A major improvement came in 1819, when Augustus Siebe invented the pressurized diving helmet, the most important feature of the modern diving suit. Siebe, a German who had come to England, designed a helmet that was a copper sphere

Kleingert's rigid metal diving suit. A regulator valve (top center) kept stale air out of the fresh-air breathing tube.

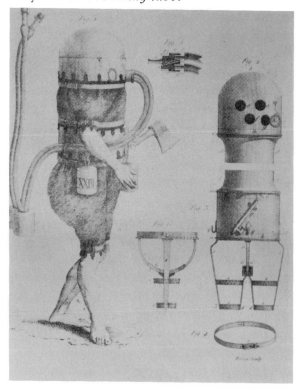

and large enough to fit comfortably over the diver's head. He chose a sphere because that shape resists the force of water pressure better than any other. A glass faceplate permitted the diver to see, and air was pumped into the helmet through a hose from the surface. In this use of a pump to supply air to the diver, Siebe was also a pioneer.

The helmet fastened onto a copper breastplate, which rode on the diver's shoulders like the shoulder pads of a football player and supported its weight. A waterproof leather jacket, riveted to the metal breastplate, reached down to the diver's hips. The air, pumped down to the diver by a surface crew, passed through the helmet and suit, escaping at the bottom of the jacket. The diver thus had a steady supply of fresh air.

What Siebe had done was to apply the principle of the diving bell to the diving suit. The helmet and jacket were, in effect, a lightweight, wearable, mini-diving bell. Even working many feet down, the diver could breathe easily because the pressure of the air that filled his lungs equaled the pressure of the water on his body.

This outfit offered more freedom of motion than any previous diving suit, and it soon became popular despite its shortcomings—one of which was that the diver could not bend over. If he did, water would rush into his helmet and drown him. Another problem was that the area in which he could work was limited by the length of his air hose. But, since divers customarily worked in a small area anyway, this was not a serious drawback.

Siebe worked hard to overcome the defects of his "open suit," so called because it was open at the bottom. By 1830 he had perfected the "closed suit," which covered the diver completely. In this model, the air escaped from an outlet valve in the helmet. By regulating the escape valve, the diver could adjust the pressure in his suit to match the depth of the water. The layer of air inside the suit also cushioned the diver and helped to insulate him against the chill of the water. With Siebe's closed suit and helmet, dives of 100 feet and more were now possible. Although there have been many technical improvements in the diving suit since then, the basic principles of Siebe's invention remain unchanged.

Bit by bit, various items were added to the basic suit and helmet as divers learned from experience. A modern helmeted diver wears a suit of heavy woolen underwear, plus one or more pairs of heavy socks, for warmth. Without this, he would lose body heat so fast that he would not be able to work for long. For work in very cold water, the underwear may be electrically heated. On top of this comes the suit itself, a one-piece outfit enclosing even his feet, with arms ending in watertight, elastic cuffs. The suit is made of tough canvas, rubberized to make it waterproof yet flexible. On his feet the diver wears lead-weighted boots to balance the heavy breastplate and helmet. Without the boots, the weight of the breastplate and helmet could easily tip him off balance and flip him upside down. There he would float, helpless to right himself. A heavy belt for holding tools goes around his waist. Lead weights are hung on the belt to counteract the buoyancy of the air inside his suit, for the diver must be heavy enough to stand firmly on the bottom. The complete outfit

Two types of diving suits used in the 1940s. The type at the right was used in relatively shallow water.

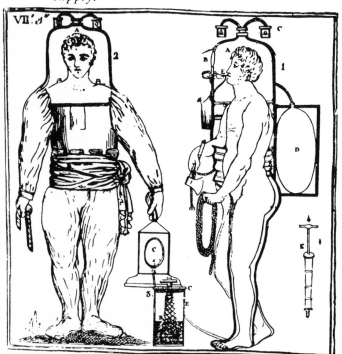

This diving apparatus, designed by Brizé-Fradin in 1808, carried a self-contained air supply.

weighs upwards of two hundred pounds.

In addition to his air hose, the diver is linked to the surface by a strong rope called a lifeline. On this he is lowered to the bottom by his tenders, or surface crew, and hauled up again when his working time is over. He can signal the surface crew by tugging on the lifeline. Often there is a telephone built into the helmet so that he can talk directly with the people topside. However, the roar of the air coming into the helmet sometimes creates so much noise that it drowns the diver's speech out; so he may end up communicating by tugs on his lifeline anyway.

There is always a danger that the diver's air hose may become kinked or fouled on some underwater object, cutting off his air supply. This danger is eliminated by a self-contained diving apparatus, in which the diver carries his own supply of air.

A model of the Drieberg diving apparatus. Bellows on diver's back, operated by moving his head, pumped air down from the surface.

Designs for self-contained diving apparatus appeared early. Well before the end of the seventeenth century, Borelli had planned one. In 1808 a Frenchman named Brizé-Fradin designed one on the same principle as Borelli's. Neither of these was ever actually tried out in practice. In 1809 another Frenchman, Frédéric de Drieberg, produced plans for a breathing apparatus which he called the Triton, after an ancient Greek sea-god. The heart of the apparatus was a bellows which was strapped to the diver's back and worked by the movement of his head. Opening the bellows sucked in air through a hose from the surface. Closing it forced air into the diver's mouth-piece. At least, it did this in theory. An illustration from a pamphlet written by Drieberg shows an added refinement. The

diver holds a candle in a waterproof lantern that appears to be supplied with air from his breathing tube. In practice, it probably would not have given enough light to help the diver in muddy water or in the dark. The idea was good, but the technology was not.

An inventor named William James designed a self-contained diving suit in 1825. Like Siebe's, it consisted of a jacket or tunic topped off by a helmet. But James held the bottom of the tunic tightly around the diver's body with an elastic belt so that air could not escape. This was necessary because the diver's air supply was limited to what he could carry in his air tank, a kind of hollow iron doughnut that went around his waist. James claimed that this would hold enough compressed air to support a diver for about one hour. The helmet was to be made of thin copper or heavy leather of the type used in shoe soles. The pressure of the diver's air supply would presumably have kept it from collapsing.

Between 1860 and 1865 two Frenchmen, a mining engineer named Benoit Rouquayrol and a navy officer named Auguste Denayrouze, collaborated on a device that was the parent of modern scuba. Called the *aérophore,* it consisted of a canister of high-pressure air with a breathing tube leading to the diver's mouth, a valve to regulate the airflow, and a metal clip to close off the diver's nose so that water could not be forced in.

On the side of the air canister was a hollow chamber whose end was closed off by a flexible metal diaphragm. One end of a short metal rod was fastened to the diaphragm; on the other end of the rod sat the

A salvage diver equipped with the Rouquayrol-Denayrouze apparatus, a forerunner of today's scuba gear.

valve, opening or closing the passage between the air canister and the chamber. The breathing tube came out of the side of the regulator chamber, so that when the diver breathed in he reduced the pressure of the air inside the chamber. The pressure of the water on the diaphragm pushed the diaphragm slightly inward, opening the valve and letting air into the regulator chamber. This pushed the diaphragm out again, and when the pressure in the regulator was equal to that of the water outside, the valve was closed. When the diver exhaled, the air escaped through a flexible rubber nozzle shaped somewhat like a duck's beak. The duck's beak also served as a safety valve to let out excess air pressure in the regulator chamber—when the diver ascended to the surface, for example. Otherwise, the pressure of the water pinched the edges of the beak together and kept it closed.

Rouquayrol had originally invented the *aérophore* for use in coal-mine disasters. With its help, rescue workers could penetrate mine tunnels filled with smoke and poisonous gases. Together, he and Denayrouze adapted the breathing apparatus for use underwater, trimming it down to about the size and weight of an army pack. The diver carried it slung like a pack from his shoulders. In practice, a surface crew pumped air down to the diver, keeping the pressure up in his canister. He could, however, disconnect the air hose and move around freely for a limited time.

The Rouquayrol-Denayrouze apparatus was not a complete success, although it was widely used. A French company, formed in 1867 to fish for sponges in the Aegean Sea, issued *aérophores* to their Greek divers. The divers may have thought that these mechanical lungs spelled unemployment for them, since one diver equipped with a breathing apparatus could do the work of a number of the old-fashioned naked divers. At any rate, they destroyed a number of the *aérophores* they were supposed to use. Professional salvage divers also disliked the apparatus, but for different reasons. They found the nose clip and mouthpiece uncomfortable and inconvenient. They much preferred the big, round helmet of Siebe's diving gear. To meet the demands of their customers, Rouquayrol and Denayrouze therefore added a helmet, while keeping the regulator mechanism. Jules Verne equipped his fictional heroes in *Twenty Thousand Leagues under the Sea* with a version of this model.

While these diving suits were used for salvage work, the first dive for scientific purposes was made in 1844 by a half-English, Belgian-born, French professor of zoology, Henri Milne-Edwards. Using a simple helmet of the Siebe type, he made a number of descents into the warm waters of the Mediterranean Sea off the coast of Sicily.

Milne-Edwards's equipment was of a very primitive design, invented by a French army officer for use in fighting fires and adapted to underwater work. Even more rudimentary than Siebe's first design, it was no more than a helmet with a cushioned bottom edge resting on the wearer's shoulders. Air bubbled out from under the edge of the helmet with every stroke of the topside pump. Sometimes, when Milne-Edwards was in a sportive mood, he would kick off his lead-soled diving boots and float to the surface like a balloon, buoyed up by his air-filled helmet.

Even with his scanty equipment, Milne-Edwards was able to learn more about undersea life than any naturalist-diver before him. Others had had to depend on specimens cast up dead on the shore or caught on a hook and line or in a net or dredge, often badly damaged in the process. Usually their specimens were further affected by being dried or preserved in alcohol. Milne-Edwards, in contrast, was able to observe sea organisms alive and uninjured. Working at depths down to twenty-five feet and remaining down for half an hour or more, he was able to note how mollusks, worms, corals, and sponges lived and grew in their natural habitats. Unfortunately, no other naturalists chose to follow Milne-Edwards's example of on-the-spot underwater observation until well after 1900.

By the late 1860s, professional divers were going quite deep. Although most diving work was done at depths of 30 to 60 feet, salvage divers on occasion went deeper, and sponge divers who accepted the idea of working with diving gear routinely went down to 80, 90, or 100 feet. Denayrouze claimed that men using his equipment could work as deep as 160 feet, while Siebe claimed a working depth of 180 feet for his diving suit.

However, strange things began to happen to divers working at depths beyond about sixty feet. Often, when they came up, they would have pains in their joints, dizziness, and nausea. Sometimes they died, like a French diver who had been sent to the Greek islands to train local sponge divers in the use of the new apparatus. That happened about 1860. A few years later (1867) twenty-four men equipped with Siebe suits were diving for sponges in the same area. Ten of them died—nearly half the group. Medical men could not determine the reason for this perplexing and dangerous phenomenon, which today is called the "bends."

The answer finally came in a roundabout way, beginning in a French coal mine, about 1840. The mine was situated near a large river, and the coal lay sixty feet down beneath a layer of water-soaked sand. Any mine shaft cut through the sand would be quickly flooded. Pumping would not work, because water was constantly leaking through the sand from the river. To solve the problem, an engineer at the mine invented the pneumatic caisson, an iron digging chamber with an open bottom, like an outsized diving bell. The caisson was pumped full of compressed air,

Underwater excavation work in a large caisson bell of the mid-1800s. It was in such caissons that workers first showed symptoms of the bends.

which kept the water down as workmen inside the big iron box scooped the dirt away.

The caisson worked beautifully, but some of the workmen complained of pains in their joints. It was blamed on their working under such damp conditions. As caissons came into general use, more and more workmen displayed these puzzling symptoms. Very often, they lost control of their muscles, staggering around like drunks. Some became paralyzed. Some died, and no one knew why.

In 1861 a graduate student named Bucquoy took a step toward solving the problem. He did a study of compressed air, based on the use made of caissons in sinking the foundations for a bridge across the Rhine River near Strasbourg, where he was studying. Bucquoy knew that gases dissolve more readily in liquids under high pressure, and he realized that the gases of the air tend to dissolve in the blood of anyone working and breathing in air under pressure. As the pressure is lowered, the dissolved gases come out of solution. If the pressure is lowered too rapidly, the dissolved gases come fizzing out, like the bubbles in a bottle of soda water when the cap is removed. Bucquoy saw that in some way this was related to the mysterious "caisson disease," and he suggested that it could be prevented by slowly reducing the pressure on the caisson workers when they came off shift, so that the dissolved gases could pass off gently and safely. At the time, Bucquoy's theory attracted little attention, for most people had not heard of caisson disease.

The very next year, 1862, caissons were used in laying the foundations for a railroad bridge over the Scorf River at Lorient. Within two months two workmen died, and an engineer was paralyzed. Medical men began to take more interest in the problem. In 1869 a French naval doctor named A. LeRoy de Méricourt took the investigation a step further. He had studied divers in the Mediterranean and the Indian Ocean, and he had come to the same conclusion as Bucquoy. But he went beyond Bucquoy in explaining the action of the gas bubbles in the bloodstream, comparing it to what happens if an air bubble gets into the bloodstream during a hypodermic injection. He used the example of a big, strong animal, a horse, being given a shot by a veterinarian. "If when giving the animal an injection," he wrote, "there is a tiny bubble in the syringe, the animal will drop as if pole-axed." He added that, if the bubble was large enough, or if there were enough

small bubbles, the horse would die. De Méricourt also looked into the case of the Greek sponge divers who had died in 1867. These men had worked at considerable depth and stayed down until they were exhausted, giving their blood ample time to soak up gases. Then, coming quickly to the surface, they suffered strange and painful attacks.

Such attacks came to be known as the bends during the building of the Brooklyn Bridge in the 1870s, when workers were contorted into fantastic postures by the agonizing pains in their joints and muscles. The man in charge of construction, Washington Augustus Roebling, was stricken by the bends himself and had to supervise the work from his sickbed.

A noted French biologist named Paul Bert undertook the first thorough, scientific study of the bends. For years he experimented with pressure chambers, learning how fast the various gases that make up the air dissolve in the bloodstream at different pressures, and how fast they come out of solution. He studied the high pressures under which divers and caisson workers labored. He also studied low pressures, such as mountain climbers and balloonists encountered. He analyzed thousands of blood samples taken at different pressures, and he discovered the cause of the bends: nitrogen. Nitrogen is a gas that makes up about 78 percent of the earth's atmosphere. Under normal conditions it is harmless. But under high pressure it dissolves in the blood, the fat, and other parts of the body. Because it needs high pressure in order to dissolve, it comes out of solution very fast when the pressure is released, faster than the body can get rid of it through the lungs. Consequently, it forms bubbles in the bloodstream and elsewhere in the body. The most common places for the bubbles to lodge are the joints, where they cause intense pain. If they block a blood vessel, the result is not only pain but convulsions. If they lodge in the spinal column, pressing on the nerves of the spinal cord, they cause paralysis. If they block one of the main blood vessels leading to or from the heart, the result is death.

Bert concluded that the way to prevent the bends was to let people who had been exposed to high pressure return to normal pressure at a slow and uniform rate, giving the nitrogen time to come out of the bloodstream slowly and gently. He also learned that the bends could be cured, if treated soon enough, by putting the victim back under high pressure and then decompressing him slowly. Bert's methods were used successfully for years until they were re-placed by an even more effective treatment developed a little after 1900 by a British scientist, John Scott Haldane.

Haldane discovered that certain people's bodies do not lose all their dissolved nitrogen under slow, uniform decompression. Enough may remain to form bubbles later. He found that he got better results by decompressing people in stages; that is, to let the pressure drop sharply by 50 percent, then have a waiting period to let the nitrogen pass out of the body before the next drop in pressure.

Haldane also worked out a series of tables for divers, specifying how long they could safely spend at any given depth and establishing the length of waiting periods at various depths on their way to the surface. These tables were adopted by the British Admiralty in 1907, and they are used, slightly modified, all over the world today.

In the 1920s, United States Navy researchers began experimenting with special breathing mixtures for very deep dives. They found that a mixture of oxygen and helium gave the best results. Helium dissolves in the body much less than nitrogen. This greatly reduces the danger of the bends. It also permits the diver's mind to function clearly, which is not always possible with ordinary compressed air, since nitrogen at high pressure has a narcotic effect. Helium does have a drawback: it is a very good heat conductor. It conducts heat away from a diver's body through the suit and into the water much more rapidly than ordinary

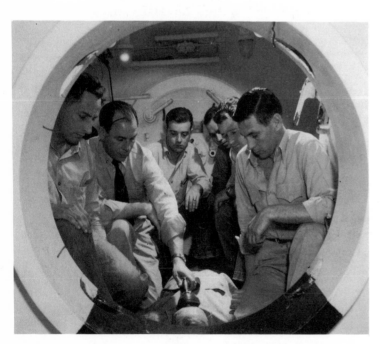

A modern decompression chamber used in training U.S. Navy divers. The doctor is demonstrating treatment of the bends.

air. Thus, divers breathing helium mixtures ran the danger of being chilled into paralysis. Electrically heated underwear largely overcame this problem. Divers using helium breathing mixtures have descended safely to 402 feet in the ocean and worked at a simulated depth of 500 feet in the navy's pressure tank. Today, helium mixtures are used routinely on deep helmet dives and by deep-ranging scuba divers.

In the early 1920s an armored diving suit with jointed arms and legs was perfected, which allowed a diver to reach depths of more than 400 feet without being crushed. In effect, the diver was a sort of one-man submersible. However, the suit severely limited the diver's freedom of motion, because it had to be built with as few joints as possible to reduce the chance of leaks. Even when the joints were made as free-moving as modern technology could manage, the pressure of the deep water (at 400 feet, about 178 pounds on every square inch of surface) squeezed them so tightly together that they tended to jam. Some of the armored diving outfits had mechanical claws at the ends of the arms so that the diver could do very simple tasks such as passing a hoisting cable around an object. But their main use was for making observations of deep-lying wrecks for salvaging. Something better was needed if deep-water work was to be effective.

An armored diving suit of the 1920s allowed divers to reach depths down to 400 feet.

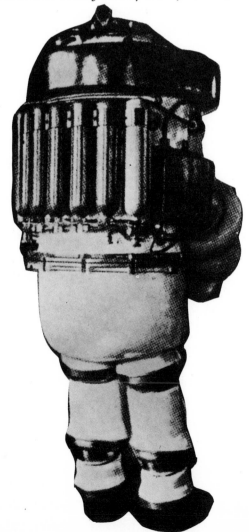
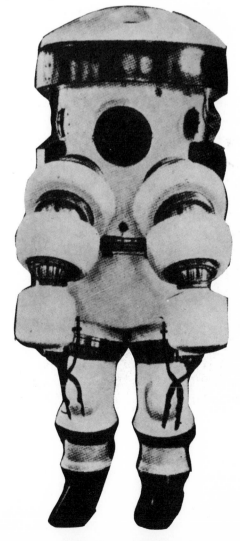

9

From Sonar and Snorkels
to Aqualungs and Atomic Submarines

MOST oceanographic research came to a halt when World War II broke out in the fall of 1939. Manpower, money, and scientific talent were needed for the war effort. But important developments did occur despite the war; in some cases, because of it.

One such development is sonar, first conceived by British scientists at the end of World War I and developed during the 1920s and 1930s, in time to play a part in World War II. Sonar was originally designed to allow surface ships to detect submerged submarines. Later it was used by submarines to locate other subs and also to measure their own distance from the ocean floor (which a submarine commander must know if he wants to avoid crashing his ship into the bottom). Today sonar is one of the oceanographer's most valuable tools. It is used for charting the sea floor, for finding schools of fish, and in guidance beacons, secured to the ocean floor, that

send out continuous sonic signals to submarines and surface vessels.

One example may give an idea of how much sonar has helped oceanographers in their work. It had always been difficult to get an accurate measurement of deep water by the traditional method of sounding. The ship had to lie still while the lead-weighted line was lowered overboard, until the bottom was finally reached, the marking knots on the line read, and then hauled in. Meanwhile, deep currents might pull the line out at an angle, making the distance to bottom appear much longer than it really was, or perhaps preventing the line from reaching bottom at all. Sometimes the waterlogged line continued to sink of its own weight, and the leadsman (the person in charge of the line) could not tell when it reached bottom. Winds and surface currents often moved the ship, distorting the reading. Even if, by luck, noth-

In a dramatic display of power, an early 1950s submarine surfaces. Advances made in World War II helped make such feats possible.

ing went wrong, a deep sounding could take an hour or more. With sonar a research ship can measure the distance in seconds.

Sonar works much like radar. A transmitter sends out impulses and the time it takes them to reach an object, bounce off, and return is measured. From this figure, the distance to the object can be calculated. Since radio waves (used for radar) can travel only a very short distance in salt water, sonar uses high-pitched sound waves. Sound travels very fast in water—about five thousand feet per second in the sea—and it travels far. In one experiment, explosions set off in Australia were picked up by scientists listening off the beaches of Bermuda, nearly twelve thousand miles away.

When a modern sonar depth-sounder sends out its high-pitched pings, electronic devices not only measure the time it takes for the echoes to return from the bottom, but also convert this data into feet, taking into account such factors as temperature and salt content of the water, which affect the speed at which the sound travels. Sonar impulses can also be transformed into light patterns on a view screen, giving a visual image of the bottom. There are also devices that trace the sonar pattern on paper, making a permanent record.

There are "side-looking" sonars that can be towed from surface vessels or mounted on submersibles to detect any objects or natural features rising from the bottom on either side of the instrument. These are useful not only in mapping the bottom, but in locating large objects such as wrecks or collapsed offshore oil-drilling platforms. And, of course, there is "forward-scanning" sonar that alerts submarines to rocks, seamounts, and unseen objects in their path, thus averting possibly fatal collisions.

The snorkel was another invention perfected during World War II. Although the idea of a tube to supply air for the engine of a submerged submarine goes back to Simon Lake's *Argonaut,* and the Dutch had used it experimentally in the 1930s, it was the German U-boats that brought it to peak efficiency. The German

snorkel was much more solidly constructed than Lake's air tube, which was simply a large hose supported by a float. If a submersible with such an air tube had attempted to travel fast, the tube would have been dragged under, flooding the engine with corrosive salt water. The German snorkel was a hollow steel mast, supported against the drag of the water in its "up" position, and hinged at its lower end to fold flat against the deck when not needed. It contained a tube for air intake and another to carry off the exhaust from the engines. A valve at the top automatically closed the tube off when a wave washed over it or if the submarine made an emergency dive. With the snorkel, a submarine could travel on its diesel engine, saving its batteries, at depths down to forty feet. The snorkel greatly extended the time that a submarine could operate submerged. No research submersibles use snorkels, however. They go far too deep, and none have internal-combustion engines.

Frogmen and midget submarines were used during World War II, and they are in turn related to the evolution of research submersibles. The frogmen were forerunners of today's scuba divers. Dressed in rubber wet suits for protection against cold, they swam beneath the surface to plant explosive charges on the hulls of enemy ships or to sabotage harbor equipment. They had swim fins on their feet to give them added speed and range. So that no trail of bubbles would betray their presence, they used a closed-circuit breathing apparatus like the Davis escape lung. Frogmen actually spent little time submerged. They approached their targets on a rubber raft, immersed to their chins,

A sea sled carries two scuba divers on an underwater mission. Such vehicles conserve divers' valuable energy and air supply.

paddling silently and concealed by the night. Only when they came within range of detection did they slip beneath the surface. English and Italian frogmen, fighting on opposite sides, scored notable successes. The Italians, who had devoted a great deal of research to submarine warfare since World War I, also developed a torpedo that was guided by a frogman, who would slip off at the last possible moment.

After the war, scuba divers developed small, torpedolike underwater vehicles, powered by batteries, that could tow them on extended dives. These vehicles were given names like "underwater scooters," "sea sleds," and "man-carrying torpedoes." Since a scuba diver can carry air enough for only about an hour and his top swimming speed is about two miles per hour,

the amount of territory he can cover under his own power is limited. The undersea vehicles, which can travel at speeds of three to four miles per hour, made it possible for divers to cover a much larger area. These vehicles could be built to travel faster, but at higher speeds the force of the water against the mask would tear it away from the diver's face. To get someplace in a hurry, a scuba diver uses a so-called "wet submersible," that is, a partly enclosed submersible that shields him from the force of the water.

Midget submarines, designed to carry one or two men, were built experimentally before World War II, and when the war broke out, several nations had small fleets of midget subs. Other nations soon followed. The midget subs had short cruising ranges since their small hulls could not hold enough batteries to supply extended power. Consequently, they were towed or carried on the deck of a bigger ship to within fifty miles of their target, and traveled only the last stretch under their own power.

Japan had a number of midget subs that were carried piggyback on larger submarines. Three were used in the attack on Pearl Harbor, but none did any damage. Japanese midget subs did sink a number of Allied ships in the Pacific, but more often than not they were unsuccessful. In fact, a number of them sank because of faulty construction.

Britain began developing midget subs in 1941 and used them in 1942 to attack Nazi warships holed up in the fjords of Norway. A standard-size submarine could not maneuver the narrow, twisting fjords with

their many unexpected shoals, but it was thought that a midget sub might have a chance. (These particular midget subs were not especially small. They measured forty feet in length, and they carried a four-man crew plus a pair of two-ton explosive charges. However, they were small in comparison to a conventional submarine's length of two to three hundred feet.)

The first attempt was not successful. Six midget subs set out to destroy three German battleships in Alta Fjord, in the far north of Norway. They were towed underwater behind regular submarines, surfacing only briefly for ventilation once every six hours. One midget sub was lost along the way when its towing cable snapped. Another developed such bad leaks that it was abandoned and scuttled by its crew. Of the remaining four, one was sunk by Ger-

A British two-man midget submarine of World War II.

man gunfire; one ran aground in the fjord when its periscope flooded; one was able to attach its explosive charges under a German battleship, causing damage but failing to sink it. The midget sub itself was damaged by the explosion and sank. The remaining sub, unable to reach its target and plagued by trouble in its electrical system, managed to escape and join its tow submarine, but had to be scuttled on the way home. Later midget sub operations, however, had greater success. An interesting feature of the British midget submarines was an air-lock chamber through which divers could leave the boat to do various tasks—attach explosive charges, cut openings in antisubmarine nets, for instance—a military adaptation of Simon Lake's air lock for salvage divers.

One of the most revolutionary inventions of the war period was not military at all. It was the aqualung, developed for sport diving in 1942 by two Frenchmen, naval officer Jacques-Yves Cousteau and mechanical engineer Emile Gagnan. Like most successful inventions, it was made possible by a long series of earlier inventions and experiments, some of them contributing in a rather roundabout way.

In part, the story goes back to the invention of diving goggles hundreds of years ago by pearl divers in the Indian and Pacific oceans. The naked human eye sees badly under water. Water is so much denser than air that light rays behave differently in it. The human eye, evolved over thousands of generations for seeing in air, cannot focus properly under water. Objects more than a few feet away are blurred and indistinct. As the diver descends, the pressure of the water pushes his eyeballs slightly out of shape and further distorts his vision. Not helpful, either, is the fact that salt water stings the eyes.

At one time, some pearl diver must have made himself a set of goggles to keep the water out of his eyes, using thin, transparent plates of tortoiseshell for the lenses. He must have found that the goggles not only kept his eyes comfortable but allowed him to see clearly, since his eyeballs were now in contact with air, not with water.

Goggles spread to other parts of the world, and glass took the place of tortoiseshell. In time, they came to be used by swimmers as well as divers. Around 1900, for instance, people attempting to swim the English Channel protected their eyes with goggles. In the 1930s, sports enthusiasts in the south of France began using goggles for hunting fish under water with the recently developed spear gun. The goggles worked well down to about twenty feet. Beyond that depth, the pressure of the water pushed the frame of the goggles rather painfully against the diver's face. At the same time, his eyeballs began to pop out, since the air inside the goggles was at normal atmospheric pressure while the water was pushing on his body with much greater pressure.

Obviously, something better was needed, and by the late 1930s the diving mask had been perfected. Because it covered the diver's nose as well as his eyes, the mask allowed the diver to equalize the air pressure inside it with that of the water by letting a little breath out into the mask. It also provided more stable vision than the goggles had, since the lenses of the goggles often went out of alignment, making the diver see double.

The final touch in skin diving was the breathing tube, known today as the snorkel. With the snorkel held in his mouth, the diver could swim or float along the surface without having to turn his head to breathe. A few years earlier, the rubber swim fin had been invented by a Frenchman. With fins, mask, and snorkel combined, the modern skin diver was born. With this simple equipment, a skin diver could make dives down to forty feet or more. On diving, an automatic valve closed off the end of his snorkel and kept water from pouring in. All that was lacking was a portable air supply.

In 1936, Cousteau was a young naval officer stationed at the big naval base of Toulon, on the Mediterranean coast of France. Like many of his friends at that time, he became addicted to skin diving. But Cousteau was not satisfied with dives of two minutes' duration, which was as long as most divers could manage on one lungful of air. There was so much to see on the bottom that he needed longer dives to explore it.

In 1938 Cousteau designed his first breathing apparatus. The armorer of his ship built it for him. It was very like the Davis escape lung, and it was very simple: a small cylinder of oxygen, an air bag made from an old motorcycle inner tube, and a gas-mask canister filled with soda lime to purify the air for rebreathing. Plus, of course, an air hose and mouthpiece. At twenty-five feet this crude, experimental apparatus worked beautifully. Cousteau decided to try it at greater depth. At forty-five feet he was delightedly observing fish when, without warning, he went into convulsions and lost consciousness. Somehow, he reached the surface and was rescued by two sailors in a rowboat, whom he had asked to keep an eye on him. Thinking that there might have been something wrong with the chemicals he used in his air purifier, he tried again the next year. He went into convulsions at the same depth. The trouble was not with Cousteau's chemicals, but with the oxygen itself. Pure oxygen is poisonous under pressure, even the pressure of water forty-five feet down. The higher the pressure, the more poisonous is the oxygen's effect. That is why deep divers do not breathe pure oxygen. They must breathe oxygen which is diluted with another gas. At three hundred feet, breathing mixtures have less than 3 percent of oxygen.

Cousteau realized that he would have to stick to ordinary compressed air, since he could not get hold of any helium. But he had no satisfactory way of controlling the flow of the air. He wanted a small, lightweight regulator device that would feed air to the diver as he needed it, something like the breathing gear used by high-altitude fliers.

Near the end of 1942 he was put in touch with Emile Gagnan, who was working on a device to feed bottled cooking gas to the engines of automobiles. (Gasoline was then practically impossible for civilians to get, since the Nazis, who had occupied France, were taking it for their army.) Cousteau explained what he was looking for, and Gagnan pulled out a small plastic valve. "Something like this?" asked Gagnan. "Our problem is somewhat the same as yours."

In a few weeks the regulator was ready, and Cousteau tested it in a river near

A scuba diver with an underwater motion picture camera.

Paris. It did not work as he had hoped. In fact, its behavior was quite puzzling. When he stood upright, air rushed out at an alarming rate. When he stood on his head, as if making a steep dive, he could hardly get air at all. Only when he swam horizontally did the air flow as it was supposed to. On the way back to Paris the two men figured out the solution to this mystifying problem. The exhaust valve was placed six inches higher than the intake valve, and the system was so sensitive that the slight difference in water pressure in these positions threw it off. When Cousteau stood up, the pressure was lower at the exhaust valve, and so the air rushed out. Head down, the pressure was higher at the exhaust valve, and this kept the air from flowing. Only when Cousteau was horizontal were the exhaust and intake on

the same pressure level, so that they could work properly. The solution was simple. They moved the parts around so that the exhaust and intake valves were right next to each other. The redesigned breathing gear worked perfectly.

Although their activities were limited by the Nazi occupation of France, Cousteau and his friends still managed to get in a good deal of diving with the aqualung. On his first test dive in the ocean, Cousteau swam into an underwater cave whose ceiling was covered with lobsters. Food was scarce in occupied France, and lobster was a prized delicacy, so he made five dives to gather lobsters for a feast, handing them up to his wife, who was floating on the surface with a mask and snorkel.

To pass the time, Cousteau and his friends explored sunken wrecks and made underwater motion pictures. They also hunted fish to fill out the scanty rations allowed them by the Germans. Cousteau and his friends learned many things on their dives. Once they observed a fishing boat dragging a trawl net over the bottom. Not only did most of the fish manage to escape the net, but the plant growth on the bottom, which gave food and shelter to so many fish and other sea organisms, was torn up and destroyed. A big piece of the sea floor had been turned into a man-made desert. Yet the fishermen in the trawler had no way of seeing how wasteful and destructive their fishing method was.

Cousteau's group gradually extended the depth of their dives to 132 feet and even farther. They planned not to stay down long enough to be endangered by the bends—nitrogen dissolves in the body

Components of an experimental heated scuba wet suit for use in cold, deep water. In left foreground is sonar equipment.

rather slowly, so that on a brief dive not enough dissolves to be dangerous. But they encountered a different danger, nitrogen narcosis, or "rapture of the depths."

At high pressure, nitrogen has a narcotic effect, and divers become intoxicated and do foolish, and even dangerous, things. Cousteau once saw a fellow diver pull out his mouthpiece and offer it to the fish. Later the diver explained that he was afraid the fish would drown if he didn't help them. Under nitrogen narcosis, a diver's senses do not function properly. He loses track of time and distance and may neglect to return to the surface before his air runs out. Sometimes he cannot tell which way is down and which is up. Some scuba divers have died from the consequences of nitrogen narcosis.

Despite the dangers of nitrogen narcosis,

oxygen poisoning, and the bends, scuba divers were freed from many disadvantages of the helmeted divers. They had no lifelines or long air hoses to foul or break; so they could swim anywhere they wanted as long as their air held out. They were not hampered by bulky, clumsy suits. Furthermore, they were not faced by two of the worst dangers to which the helmeted diver is prey: squeeze and blowup.

Squeeze occurs when the diver loses pressure in his suit. It can happen if his air pump at the surface stops working, or if he falls off the side of a wreck into deeper water. In its mildest form, the squeeze, or sudden pressure of the sea, forces the blood from the diver's body into his head (the region of lowest pressure), rupturing the blood vessels of his brain and killing him. Under greater pressure differentials, it can strip the flesh from his bones and force it into his helmet.

Blowup, or ballooning, is the opposite of squeeze. It happens when the pressure inside the diver's suit builds up too high, usually because his air outlet valve is not functioning properly, but sometimes because of carelessness. Before he knows it, the diver's suit is inflated so that his arms and legs stick out like rigid sausages. He cannot move his arms to reach the outlet valve and let the air out. At the same time, he becomes so buoyant that he goes rocketing up to the surface. Under the lower pressure at the surface, his suit may burst open, and he may sink and drown before his tenders can haul him in to safety. In any case, he must be rushed to a decompression chamber to stave off the bends.

The aqualung diver avoids these dangers because he has no pressurized suit that can blow up like a balloon. And his breathing regulator keeps the pressure inside his lungs just equal to the pressure of the water on his body.

After the war, the French navy appointed Cousteau head of an underwater research group. He and his associates improved the design of masks, suits, and other equipment. They hunted down mines left over from the war. They photographed a French submarine laying mines and firing a torpedo. They experimented with the effects of underwater explosions on divers. Then they became involved with underwater archaeology, one of their most fascinating ventures.

A crippled diver told a member of the group, Frederic Dumas, about a spot where hundreds of lobsters lived near some old pots. On investigation, these turned out to be ancient Greek and Roman wine jars called *amphorae*. They were part of the cargo of a Greek ship that had gone down about 230 B.C. Also in the cargo was a neatly packed shipment of dinner plates, each bearing identical marks from a mold. The marks showed that the ancient Greeks had mass production methods in at least one industry. This was new information to archaeologists. The divers also brought up pieces of lead sheathing from the hull, bronze and copper spikes, and even fragments of wood, all of which provided valuable new clues about Greco-Roman shipbuilding.

The group explored many other wrecks, following hints from local fishermen whose nets sometimes brought up ancient-looking objects. They found a great variety of objects. On one dive they even found prefabricated sections of marble columns,

presumably being shipped from workshops in Greece to outlying colonies in western North Africa or southern France.

Cousteau was one of the first to make systematic archaeological explorations of sunken ships. Although not an archaeologist himself, he took archaeologists on his projects to guide the work of recovery. Divers had located ancient wrecks before, but their concern had been simply to rescue sculptures and other valuable objects, without noting where or how they lay or making a plan of the ship—details which an archaeologist must know if he is to make a worthwhile study.

By the early 1950s, Cousteau had become one of the world's leading authorities on scuba diving and underwater exploration. His books and films, and those of his associates, have made millions of people aware of the marvelous world that lies beneath the sea. Cousteau has probably done more for underwater research than any other individual, even Beebe. Beebe opened up vast new realms to science, but he needed a costly bathysphere, a support ship, and a sizable crew in order to do it. Cousteau made the underwater world accessible to anyone who could spare a few dollars to rent a scuba outfit.

After the war, Cousteau's group made successively deeper dives to learn how far a scuba diver could go. They found that about 300 feet was the limit for an experienced diver in good condition, while 120 feet was the safe limit for an amateur. It was clear that for exploring the depths the diver must be protected by some sort of rigid, incompressible container. The bathysphere gave protection to the observer, but its range was too limited.

A Navy diver in a wet suit leaves the water after a training dive with experimental deep-water equipment.

In 1948, a new type of deep-sea research craft was launched, the bathyscaphe (Greek for "deep boat"). It was the invention of Auguste Piccard, a Swiss professor of physics who was famous for his balloon ascents into the stratosphere. He wanted to descend to 13,000 feet, and to do this he needed a vessel like Beebe's bathysphere, but stronger. And he did not trust a steel cable to hold a massive steel chamber at that depth, for the cable might break of its own weight. Furthermore, the whiplash effect of the cable, which had given Beebe so much trouble at a few hundred feet, would be greatly increased at 13,000 feet.

Piccard decided on a free-diving vessel that could return to the surface under its own buoyancy, and he combined the ideas of the bathysphere and the balloon. Just as an aerial balloon has a gas bag, Piccard's underwater balloon had a huge float made of thin sheet metal and filled with gasoline. Gasoline is lighter than water and does not mix with it; so the gasoline gave buoyancy. It is also nearly incompressible, so it would keep the float from being crushed by the increasing water pressure as the boat sank. A heavy load of ballast would give him the weight he needed to descend. When he reached the depth he wanted, Piccard planned to halt his descent by releasing part of his ballast, as a balloonist does to keep his balloon from falling. He would then stabilize it by alternately releasing small quantities of gasoline and ballast—a delicate balancing operation but one that he was used to from his famous balloon ascents of the 1930s. A pair of electric motors would propel the bathyscaphe horizontally for short observation excursions.

Piccard had actually begun work on the bathyscaphe in 1937, supported by a grant from the Belgian National Scientific Research Fund. But the German occupation of Belgium early in World War II cut the project short in the planning stage. He continued the work after the war, but shortages and inflation forced him to skimp on some details of the construction. The finished bathyscaphe was named FNRS-2, from the initials of the Belgian fund that had paid for it. It was ready for testing in the fall of 1948.

The bathyscaphe's test run was an international project. The French Navy had lent support, and Cousteau and his aqua-lung divers assisted in the preparations. The Cousteau group also contributed a mechanical claw, of their own design, for taking samples of rocks from the bottom.

Another attachment for the sphere was a seven-barreled harpoon gun invented by Piccard and a Belgian physicist, Max Cosyns, and operated by water pressure. The harpoon gun was to capture specimens of giant squids or other large underwater animals for study. The harpoons had electrical-shock heads to stun the "sea monsters"; if that did not work, the harpoon gave the animal a lethal injection of strychnine. As it turned out, neither attachment was used.

Inside the sphere were dozens of instruments, including a Geiger counter for measuring cosmic rays. The air purification system was planned to support two men for twenty-four hours. In case the bathyscaphe drifted out of reach of its support ship while submerged, it had a radar mast to broadcast signals as soon as it reached the surface. This was necessary because there was no way for the occupants of the sphere to open it up from the inside.

The first dive was made by Piccard and a French scientist. It was a shallow dive, in eighty feet of water. Though it lasted only sixteen minutes, the men had to sit inside the sphere for three hours while ten thousand gallons of gasoline were pumped into the float. They could only enter the sphere while the bathyscaphe was high and dry on the deck of its support ship, but the float could not be filled on deck because of the danger of explosion. In addition, once filled, it would have been too heavy to hoist over the side.

An amusing incident occurred on this dive. The final loads of ballast were poured into their holders by a French crewman standing on top of the float. He stayed at his post until he had sunk up to his neck in the water, then swam clear. Seconds later, the bathyscaphe surfaced again. The man's own weight had meant the difference between the bathyscaphe's sinking and floating. While everyone except the two scientists in the sphere enjoyed a good laugh, enough ballast was added to make up the difference in weight, and the seven-foot white sphere and its float descended. When it rose again, the crew needed five hours to pump the gasoline out and hoist the bathyscaphe back on board so that the two men inside could be released from their cramped quarters.

The next dive was an unmanned one, with an automatic timer set to release the ballast. Piccard had planned to send the bathyscaphe down in the early morning, giving it plenty of time to sink, but various mishaps delayed the launching until four o'clock in the afternoon. The scheduled time for ballast release was 4:40. The timer was sealed in the sphere, down under the water, and no one could get at it without ruining the entire experiment. Reluctantly, Piccard gave the order to let go, and the bathyscaphe disappeared. The surface crew watched as anxiously as Piccard for its reappearance. If anything went wrong, undersea exploration would be set back by many years.

The bathyscaphe did surface, much to everyone's relief. But it was in sorry shape. The radar mast had vanished. Worse yet, waves at the surface battered the big float, buckling it badly. The thin metal skin of the float was billowing in and out, threatening to spring a leak. A bad storm blew up, preventing the crew from attaching hoses to pump out the gas. Reluctantly the order was given to blow the gasoline compartments clear with carbon dioxide. By the time the exhausted crew got the FNRS-2 back on board, the thin metal skin of the float was badly torn, and the sphere had lost one of its motors and propellers. The inside of the sphere was in perfect condition, however, and its depth recorder read forty-five hundred feet. Thus the bathyscaphe was at least a partial success. However, the Belgians blamed Piccard for attracting the whole world's attention to a project they felt was an embarrassing failure. They refused to give the foreign scientist—until recently their hero—any more help.

After nearly two years of haggling between governments and bureaucrats, the French Navy agreed to rebuild FNRS-2 in return for official possession of it. A new float was designed, which was not only strong enough to stand up to the pounding

of waves but was boat-shaped, so that it could be towed between dives instead of riding on the deck of a mother ship. (The original float was shaped like a giant, oval canned ham and was not at all seaworthy.) In addition, the sphere was remodeled with an entry tower, so that the observers could enter or leave it at any time when the bathyscaphe was at the surface.

But during the reconstruction, French naval engineers refused to consult with Piccard and ignored his suggestions as much as possible, just as U.S. naval engineers had ignored John Holland half a century earlier. Deeply offended, Piccard resigned from the project and raised funds to construct another bathyscaphe, which he named *Trieste* in honor of the place where it was to be built. Both the *Trieste* and the FNRS-3, which was taken over by Cousteau's group, made highly successful dives, setting new records and making valuable observations.

Otis Barton made a brief return to oceanographic diving in 1949, with a redesigned version of the bathysphere which he called the Benthoscope. In this chamber, which had an additional window in the floor, he descended to 4,500 feet off the coast of California, setting a temporary record for the world's deepest manned descent. The dive provided no information of use to biologists, for Barton was not a naturalist and could not identify the animals he saw. Over his telephone intercom, Barton told reporters that he wished Beebe were with him. He made some fragmentary sketches, but they were too incomplete to be helpful. However, he did prove that the bathysphere's limit could be surpassed, and he made useful contributions

Trieste-I swings from its loading crane. Beneath the striped, sausage-shaped float is the pressure-proof passenger sphere.

to the design of windows for deep-ranging observation vessels.

The *Trieste* shattered Barton's record four years later, though not without some preliminary trouble. The *Trieste*'s sphere was the same size as that of the ill-fated FNRS-2, with an inside diameter of six feet seven inches. This gave the occupants a chance to stand up and stretch, a great relief on a long dive. The float was more than twice as big as the earlier bathyscaphe's, holding up to twenty-five thousand gallons of gasoline. As a safety measure, it was divided into twelve separate compartments, plus two water tanks to be flooded for submerging. The ballast load was nine tons of steel shot. It was held in two large tubs with electrically controlled release valves. The tubs themselves were held to the forty-nine-foot float by electromagnets, so that in an emergency the whole load could be dumped, freeing the bathyscaphe to float up. The windows of the sphere were wide, cone-shaped pieces of Plexiglas plastic, six inches thick. Under pressure, the plastic yielded slightly but did not break, as did glass or quartz. Like FNRS-2, *Trieste* had electric motors to navigate along the bottom.

After several shallow test dives in the Gulf of Naples, Piccard and his son Jacques took the *Trieste* on its first deep-sea dive. The depth sonar had not yet been installed, so they could not judge the speed at which they were approaching the bottom. Before they knew it, the sphere sank four and one half feet deep into mud. The depth gauge read 3,570 feet. Unable to see anything, the Piccards jettisoned their ballast, and in a few minutes the *Trieste* was light enough to float free. Professor Piccard strained for a glimpse of the ocean floor as they lifted off, hoping to see living organisms that no human being had ever seen before. But his hopes were thwarted, for the sphere stirred up an impenetrable cloud of mud as it pulled free. A little over a month later (September 30, 1953), the father-and-son team took the *Trieste* down to 10,300 feet. This time, everything functioned properly.

Meanwhile, the French were making a series of deep dives with FNRS-3, piloted by two navy officers named Georges Houot and Pierre Willm. By chance, the dives were scheduled so that the French Navy and Piccard seemed to be in a vengeful competition (in fact, they were not). Early in 1954 FNRS-3 reached 13,284 feet in the Atlantic off the western bulge of Africa. This record stood until 1960.

Much more was accomplished on these dives than merely setting depth records. The bathynauts conducted experiments with sound and light waves. They took samples of the bottom. They measured variations in the temperature and salt content of the water, and took samples for chemical analysis. They observed the life-forms of the deep waters and took photographs to back up their observations.

On their early dives, the bathynauts sometimes encountered unexpected problems. For instance, Piccard was stopped by a layer of cold, dense water about forty feet off the bottom. To sink through it, he had to reduce his buoyancy somehow. He could either wait until his gasoline cooled down to the temperature of this layer and contracted; let some of the gasoline go; or return to the surface for more ballast. Since this was a practice dive and not particularly urgent, he chose the third alternative. The Frenchmen in FNRS-3 had the opposite experience. After a long submergence, they let go some ballast, but the bathyscaphe refused to rise. The gasoline in the float had become chilled, shrunk in volume, and lost buoyancy. Releasing more ballast brought them up safely, however.

Although the bathyscaphe dives produced few sensational discoveries—so the public quickly lost interest—their observations were of great value to oceanographers. As far as scientists were concerned, the bathyscaphes were more than paying their way.

While Piccard and the French were setting new depth records, work was under way on a military project that had important results for undersea exploration. In 1955 the U.S.S. *Nautilus,* the world's first nuclear-powered submarine, was launched. It made voyages of unbelievable length without once coming to the surface, and in 1958 it crossed the North Pole under the ice. The commander noted the water temperature, 32.4° F., and the depth of the water, 13,410 feet by the ship's sonar. The *Nautilus*'s sister nuclear submarines followed this spectacular performance with new records of their own, and in 1959 the *Skate* crashed through the ice to surface at the North Pole. Previously, the *Triton* had traveled entirely around the world submerged, making the voyage in eighty-four days. The publicity generated by these remarkable exploits revived public interest in the underwater world. Perhaps more important, it made the navy aware of the need for widespread studies of the geography of the sea bottom and of

Nuclear submarine with its missile firing tubes open.

ocean currents not yet charted. Divers could not make such studies, and surface ships could do them only imperfectly. But if a deep-ranging submersible fitted for making observations could be developed . . .

The nuclear submarine Whale *surfaces through thick Arctic ice at the North Pole.*

10

Modern Research Submersibles

FRANCE and the United States were the first nations to become aware of the usefulness of research submersibles, and they were the first to devote government funds to developing them. Once government support was available, manned research submersibles were not long in coming. In fact, men had been planning them for some time. In the early 1950s Cousteau had made plans for carrying on his undersea explorations at depths far beyond those a diver could reach. In 1955 his group began work on the design of a vehicle that could take observers down to the thousand-foot level while maintaining them at a comfortable sea-level atmospheric pressure. In 1959 Cousteau's group had a two-man submersible ready for action.

It had an unusual shape, neither a sphere like a bathyscaphe hull nor a cigar like a submarine. From the side it looked like a flattened sphere or a bulging pan-cake. Because of its shape, Cousteau nicknamed it *Soucoupe Plongeante,* which is French for *Diving Saucer*. At the time, newspapers were full of reports of "flying saucers" from outer space visiting the earth, and it may have tickled Cousteau's sense of humor to imagine a "saucer" exploring the inner space of the ocean depths. In some ways outer space and the ocean depths are very much alike. Both are regions which human beings could not reach until less than half a man's lifetime ago. In both, conditions are extremely different from those on the earth's surface, so different that men cannot survive there without elaborate protection.

Cousteau thought that a research submersible should be able to do almost everything that a scuba diver could do. Therefore, it should be small and easily maneuverable; it should give the observers inside it a good view of the ocean; and it should have some sort of mechanical arm for gathering samples of rock, bottom ooze, and marine life. It should also have a camera for making a visual record of things that are observed on the dive, and possibly even picking up phenomena that the human observers may have missed.

These ideas were realized in the *Diving Saucer*. It was small—only nine feet across and five feet high. On the inside it was six and one half feet long and four feet wide, giving the occupants plenty of room to stretch out, for Cousteau also believed in being comfortable. Due to the strong design of its hull, the *Diving Saucer* could reach a safe depth of 1,350 feet.

The pilot and the observer lay on their stomachs on couches, looking out through their viewports. A camera mounted between them shot a central view. Under the "chin" of the craft was a mechanical arm ending in a clamshell scoop. Although it appeared clumsy, this scoop was so deli-

Checking out Cousteau's Diving Saucer *aboard the support vessel, a crewman grasps one of the* Saucer's *propulsion jets.*

cately controlled that it could gather fragile specimens such as the intricately branched basket star (a type of starfish) without damaging them.

The *Diving Saucer* was propelled by water jets, one on each side of the hull. The jet nozzles could be angled up or down for maneuvering. A two-horsepower electric motor drove the pumps for the jets, giving a top speed of a little over one mile per hour. This may seem very slow considering that cars travel sixty-five or seventy miles an hour on a freeway and airliners reach an airspeed of four to five hundred miles per hour. But it is more than fast enough for scientists who want to study and photograph the life-forms of the sea floor. For these purposes, high speed is a disadvantage, whisking observers past fish and sea fans and sponges before they are able to get a good look.

French scientists were not overly impressed with the *Diving Saucer* when Cousteau began demonstrating it. But its performance made a big impression on a visiting American scientist. He told management at the Westinghouse Electric Corporation about the highly maneuverable little submersible. (Westinghouse was already involved in undersea developments through making torpedoes for the United States Navy.) The result was that Cousteau agreed to design and build for Westinghouse a larger submersible of the same type that would be capable of reaching a much greater depth. This submersible was named *Deepstar-4000*, since 4,000 feet was its rated depth capability. (Depth capability is the technical term for the maximum depth at which an undersea vessel can work safely.)

While construction was proceeding on *Deepstar,* Westinghouse leased the *Diving Saucer* from Cousteau and brought it to California to demonstrate to West Coast scientists how useful a submersible could be in studying marine biology and other aspects of oceanography. A number of scientists pooh-poohed the idea at first, suspecting that a submersible was just an ineffectual gimmick. One dive was enough to show them how wrong they were.

During the winter of 1964/1965 the *Saucer* made over one hundred dives in the Pacific, permitting scientists to investigate such diverse phenomena as the life of the sea floor and mud slides in deep underwater canyons. One important project was a study of the Deep Scattering Layer, a mysterious layer in the water that reflects sonar signals, thus giving false depth readings. During World War II, navy men were frequently baffled by the Deep Scattering Layer, which would give very shallow sonar readings where the charts said there was water thousands of feet deep. The treacherous Deep Scattering Layer would not even stay in one place—it rose toward the surface at nightfall and sank back toward the depths at the first sign of light.

Scientists had some theories about what the Deep Scattering Layer might be composed of. Biologists diving in the *Trieste* and other bathyscaphes had found dense concentrations of fish, shrimps, and jellyfish at certain levels in the sea, which seemed to correspond pretty closely with the readings that surface ships reported. They believed that sonar signals could be reflected by these organisms, giving misleading readings. However, the bathy-

scaphes sank too rapidly for the biologists to identify with any certainty the organisms they saw. They were like people on an express train trying to pick faces out of the crowd as they rushed past a station.

With a submersible, which can hover at one level, scientists can make close observations. Studies done with the *Diving Saucer* found two separate Deep Scattering Layers at different depths, one composed mainly of fish and the other mainly of jellyfish. (Studies in other parts of the world have proved that many different organisms can make up a sound-reflecting layer. These were the ones found off the coast of Mexico.)

Deepstar-4000, completed in 1964, was used chiefly for scientific dives. It was followed by *Deepstar-2000,* launched in 1969, which was designed for utility dives, such as checking on submarine cables and pipelines, along the continental shelf. *Deepstar-20,000,* the third of the series, was designed for exploration of the deep abyssal sea floors down to 20,000 feet. The figure of 20,000 feet has a special importance to oceanographers, for more than 90 percent of the sea floor of the entire world lies above this depth. A submersible that can work at a depth of 20,000 feet can thus reach more than nine-tenths of the world's ocean floor, whether for investigating life-forms, taking geological samples, prospecting for oil or ores, or for military purposes.

Deepstar-20,000 never reached its target depth. For lack of funds, it was put into storage in 1970, before construction was completed. Except for the bathyscaphes, only one manned submersible so far has dived to 20,000 feet, the specially con-

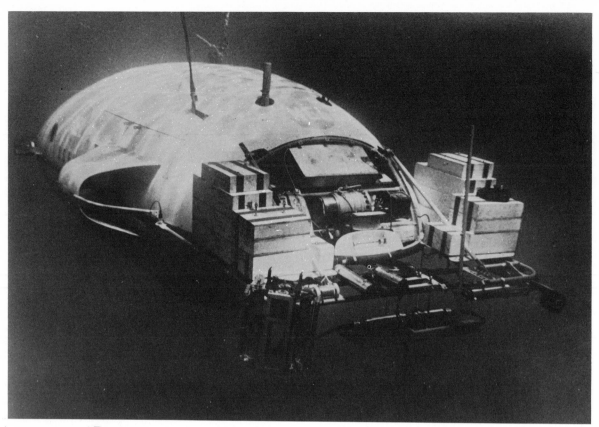

A stern view of Deepstar-4000.

structed French Navy submersible *Archimède*.

The first undersea vessel to reach the 20,000-foot mark was the bathyscaphe *Trieste*. In fact, *Trieste* far exceeded that depth in 1960, when it reached a depth of 35,800 feet below sea level, the lowest known spot on the earth's surface, in the Marianas Trench, a deep gash in the floor of the western Pacific. The location had been pinpointed by navy sonar ships. For this dive, the *Trieste* was outfitted with a new, stronger sphere forged by the great German steelmaker Krupp. The new sphere had walls 4¾ inches thick and weighed 14.3 tons, three tons more than the original sphere. To handle the additional weight, the float was lengthened by 8 feet.

The project was sponsored by the United States Navy, which had bought the *Trieste*. The pilot on the big dive was Jacques Piccard, and the observer was Lieutenant Don Walsh of the Navy. For some reason, navy bureaucrats had not wished Piccard to take part in the dive, perhaps wanting navy personnel to have all the glory. Piccard, for whom this dive was the culmination of his life's work, appealed in vain. Not until he pointed to a certain clause in his contract did the navy relent.

One of the biggest questions facing the two men was whether they would find animal life at such a depth. Deep-sea life is limited not only by cold and pressure, but by lack of food, for plants cannot grow in the darkness of the depths, and the bottom-dwelling animals have to live either on the scattering of dead organisms that rains down on them from above—or on each other. Early nineteenth-century biologists had stated that life could not exist in the depths of the sea. But then submarine telegraph cables were laid in several thousand feet of water. When these were later fished up for repair, they were often found covered with sponges and other sea animals that do not swim or crawl. Since these animals cannot move about, they could not possibly have attached themselves to the cable as it was hauled up. They had to have grown on it in the depths. Some, in fact, had grown completely around the cable. Science had to revise its ideas in the face of the facts.

Bit by bit, the known limit of life in the depths was rolled back. H.M.S. *Challenger,* on its great oceanographic voyage around the world in 1873–1875, dredged up live specimens from 15,000 feet and even deeper. Later oceanographic expeditions found life at increasingly greater depths. The Danish research ship *Galathea,* in the early 1950s, recovered sea anemones, shellfish, sea cucumbers, and a bristle worm from 32,500 feet. But some oceanographers doubted that Piccard and Walsh would find life in the valley in the bottom of the Marianas Trench for which they were headed. They thought the water in such a depression would probably be isolated from oxygen-bearing currents, and therefore would be too low in oxygen to support life.

As Piccard was bringing the bathyscaphe to a landing, he looked down at the flat, ivory-colored expanse of the bottom. Just below the sphere he saw a foot-long flatfish illuminated by his searchlight. The fish stared at the sphere and then swam slowly away. A little later, he saw a red shrimp swim past his viewport. The question of life in the deepest part of the ocean had been answered.

The *Trieste* played another important role in 1963, when it located and photographed the wreckage of the nuclear submarine *Thresher.* The *Thresher* had disappeared mysteriously on a test dive off the coast of New England, and the navy was searching frantically for traces of the lost sub. Surface vessels equipped with sonar and remote-control cameras on cables had swept the area, but the bottom was too rough to allow sonar to detect the remains of the *Thresher,* and the range of a camera was too limited. Only the *Trieste* could go deep enough for a close-range search of the bottom.

On its third dive, the bathyscaphe found a plastic protective shoe of the type worn by sailors on nuclear subs. On another dive, it found and photographed a two-mile trail of debris that led to the *Thresher*'s hull, 8,400 feet down. It also retrieved a piece of pipe marked with the *Thresher*'s identification number.

After ten years of diving, the *Trieste* was showing signs of wear and tear. So the navy rebuilt it, using Piccard's original sphere and a new, streamlined float for easier towing. The remodeled bathyscaphe, named *Trieste II,* continued the investigation of the *Thresher*'s wreckage over the summer of 1964. In 1969 it performed another sad mission, locating the wreck of the U.S.S. *Scorpion,* a nuclear submarine which had sunk in the Atlantic Ocean in 10,000 feet of water. *Trieste II* can go as deep as 20,000 feet, but so far it has not been called upon to make so deep a dive.

Even before *Deepstar-4000* was finished, submersibles by other builders began to appear. By the late 1960s probably more than a hundred submersibles had

Trieste-II *located wreckage of the nuclear sub* Thresher. *Boat-shaped float enables* Trieste-II *to be towed.*

been built. The largest builder and user of submersibles was the United States, but France, Japan, Russia, and Canada were also active. Germany and Britain had a few submersibles each, and South Africa was planning one to search the seabed for diamonds. The peak of submersible construction and activity was from 1965 to 1970, after which a widespread economic recession forced many countries to curtail their programs.

Submersibles vary so greatly in size and design, depending on the purposes for which they are intended, that it is almost impossible to give a general description of them. However, most of them, like a submarine, have an inner "pressure hull" that holds the crew and an outer hull exposed

The "anatomy" of the bathyscaphe Trieste-II.

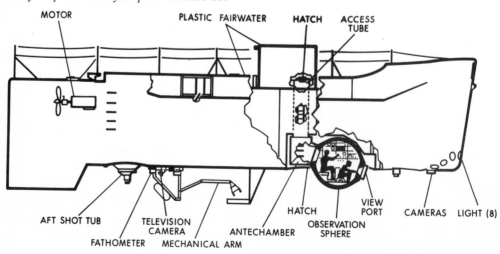

BATHYSCAPH TRIESTE II

to the water. All of them are very different from surface vessels. In fact, the submersibles that perform best underwater are quite unseaworthy on the surface.

Since the outer hull of a submersible does not have to stand up against the pressure of the water, it is usually made of some light material, like thin metal or fiber glass. The outer hull's purpose is to reduce drag, shield the batteries, motors, and other equipment located outside the pressure hull, and prevent them from becoming snagged.

Steel is the chief material used for pressure hulls, but aluminum, Plexiglas (acrylic plastic), and titanium have also been used, singly or in combination. Special high-strength steels developed for use in atomic subs and in the space program are used in submersibles. One such steel can stand a load of 300,000 pounds per square inch. Unfortunately, the stronger the steel, the harder it is to weld. Moreover, welding weakens the steel by changing its crystal structure.

Aluminum has the advantage of being much lighter than steel and still relatively strong. It shares the disadvantage of being difficult to weld, and it is also corroded by seawater, particularly under high pressure. The builders of *Aluminaut,* the best-known aluminum-hulled submersible, solved the corrosion problem by giving the metal six coats of plastic paint. The welding problem was sidestepped by using bolts to hold the sections of the hull together. Flexible gaskets of synthetic rubber or similar material were used between the sections. The deeper the submersible went, the tighter the water pressure pushed the joints together, so that

leaking was never a problem. A number of submersibles use mechanical clamps to hold their hulls together.

Acrylic plastic was used for the viewports in Auguste Piccard's FNRS-2, and it has been the standard material for submersible windows since then. Around 1960, an American scientist proposed building an entire submersible of the transparent material, giving the occupants unlimited visibility around them. By 1971 three acrylic-hulled submersibles had been built and operated in the United States: the United States Navy's *Nemo* and *Makakai* and the Smithsonian Institution's *Johnson-Sea-Link.* These are all sphere-shaped, with no outer hull that would interfere with freedom of vision. Acrylic is light, strong, and buoyant. Submersible designers think it is best adapted for use down to the 1,000-foot level. Beyond that depth, an acrylic hull must be made so thick that it loses its advantages of buoyancy.

Before the Space Age, titanium was chiefly used as a white pigment in paints. When the space race between Russia and America began, rocket and missile designers found new uses for the light, strong, relatively rare metal, which weighs about 25 percent less than aluminum. Later, it was used successfully in submersibles. *Alvin,* for example, now has titanium buoyancy spheres and a titanium hull to enable it to dive to 12,000 feet. Jacques Piccard has plans for a titanium-hulled submersible to reach the 20,000-foot level.

Glass may seem a strange choice for a vessel which is subjected to the tremendous pressures of the deep sea. It is a brittle substance, easily shattered by a sharp blow.

Aluminaut *has an estimated depth limit of 8,000 feet. Built of aluminum, it holds three persons (more for a short dive).*

The plastic-hulled submersible Makakai. *Fast and maneuverable, it was designed especially for observing sharks and porpoises.*

But glass can withstand astonishingly heavy pressure as long as the pressure is steady. This property has been known for many years. A favorite exhibition stunt of glass companies was to have an elephant stand on a thick sheet of glass supported between two beams. Glass spheres have been used to bring up samples from depths as great as 20,000 feet since about 1960. Occasionally a glass float failed, due to stresses in the glass, but this has rarely happened. In 1971 the United States Navy completed a part-glass submersible named *Deep View,* designed for an operating depth of 1,500 feet.

It is difficult to produce large pieces of glass that are free of internal stresses. Therefore, designs for glass-hulled submersibles call for hemispheres or smaller sections, bonded at the edges with some flexible sealer and held together by a metal framework. As with other segmented hulls, the greater the water pressure, the tighter the joint.

Deep-ranging submersibles usually have hulls that are so heavy they need extra buoyancy. Since hollow tanks would be crushed by the pressure of the depths, a material called syntactic foam is used. It is made of millions of tiny, hollow glass bubbles embedded in plastic. Ordinary foam plastic would be crushed flat by the sea at the depths these craft must reach, but the syntactic foam resists crushing.

Submersibles are designed with a large safety factor, ranging from $1\frac{1}{2}$ or 2 to 1 for most metal-hulled craft to 4 to 1 for hulls of other materials. The safety factor is the ratio between the depth the vessel is designed for and the depth at which it will actually collapse. For example, *Alvin*'s original rated depth limit was 6,000 feet;

its collapse depth was calculated at 16,000 feet, a safety factor of 2⅔ to 1. Thus, in case of an accident, a submersible can go beyond its rated depth without being crushed. As an extra safeguard, a submersible can gain buoyancy by dropping ballast weights, batteries, or other equipment and so float safely to the surface.

During construction, machines test the pressure hull before the rest of the equipment is added on. The machines place a very high pressure on the hull while sensors attached at various points measure the stresses showing in the hull's material. From these data the testers can calculate the breaking strength of the hull without actually destroying it. Once a smashup did occur in a testing lab. A spare hull made for *Alvin* was placed in a pressure chamber, and the pressure turned on. The 6,000-foot operating level pressure was reached and passed. But the tester's instructions were to find the ultimate crushing point of the steel sphere, so he increased the pressure to the 9,000-foot mark, and past it. Suddenly there was a rending crash. The pressure chamber had exploded! *Alvin*'s

The pressure hull of the DSRV (foreground) is three joined spheres. In background is the streamlined outer hull.

hull was still in one piece. However, in practice it is not safe to rely on a pressure hull's being so much stronger than the rated depth limit. The pressure of the depths, combined with the low temperature, can have unpredictable effects upon materials. Metals develop flaws and crack apart. Some plastics, almost indestructible on dry land, crumble to powder in the depths.

As mentioned earlier, the ideal hull shape from the standpoint of strength is the sphere. But a sphere of a practical size can hold only two or three persons. To increase the capacity of the submersible, two or more spheres can be joined together, connected by short tunnels, and held in place by a framework. The sphere is still the best choice for the pressure hull for extreme depths, and because a sphere shape is difficult to maneuver, the outer hull can give the submersible the streamlined shape it needs for maneuverability.

A cylindrical inner hull is more convenient for its occupants than a sphere is, and it is much easier to maneuver through the water. However, it is not as strong. Designers therefore try to retain some of the sphere's strength by using hemispheres (half spheres) for the ends of the cylinder and by stiffening its body with ring-shaped ribs.

With very few exceptions, research submersibles are battery-powered. (The chief exceptions are the United States Navy's nuclear-powered *NR-1* and diesel-electric *Dolphin*.) Most submersibles use the lead-acid type of battery, which is like an automobile battery. Some use silver-zinc batteries, which are very expensive but longer lasting than ordinary batteries, and are

A specially designed crane lifts the Diving Saucer *from the water.*

much more powerful weight for weight. But even the best batteries must be recharged frequently, and so the cruising range of a submersible is quite limited. As a rule, the smaller the submersible, the fewer batteries it can carry and the shorter its cruising range is.

A fuel cell, which converts the heat of burning fuel directly into electricity, would be the ideal power source for a research submersible. If hydrogen were used as the fuel, the only product of combustion would be harmless water. Scientists have been trying to develop a fuel cell that could deliver a usable quantity of power to a submersible's motors, but so far they have not succeeded. One small submersible, *Star I,* was powered by a fuel cell. Its successors were battery-powered, however.

Many submersibles do not have rudders or diving planes. At their slow cruising speeds, these steering devices are ineffec-

tive. Instead, they may have a tiltable propeller, or they may maneuver with the aid of additional propellers, called thrusters, that push them up or down, left or right. Some advanced submersibles have a "mercury-trim" system, in which mercury is pumped between tanks at the front and rear to tilt the submersible's nose up or down.

Because of their limited range and slow speed, submersibles must have a "mother ship" to transport them to the worksite and back again. Most mother ships are small converted warships or cargo ships fitted with a heavy-duty crane to swing the submersible over the side and back up on deck when its work is done. However, in a rough sea the mother ship may pitch and roll so much that the submersible, dangling at the end of its lifting cable, is in danger of smashing into the side of the ship, with catastrophic results. In bad

Star III, *with a sonar receiver dish and "pingers" mounted on its nose.*

Perry's research submersible PC-8 is fitted with a bottom-sampling device.

weather, therefore, the submersible may have to be towed. This is really a last-ditch measure. Submersibles are not designed for stability on the surface of the water, particularly in stormy weather, and they can get bounced around badly enough to damage delicate equipment.

Submersibles carry a bewildering variety of equipment, depending on the jobs they are designed to do. In addition to depth-measuring sonar, they may have forward- and side-scanning sonar. This is particularly important for operation at depths beyond the range of visible light. Nearly all of them have underwater sonic telephones for communication with the surface. They may have TV and motion picture cameras, still cameras, and searchlights to make photography possible and permit human eyes to see. In the late 1960s navy scientists invented an underwater laser searchlight that produced a blue green beam—the wavelength of light that travels best under water. According to reports, the laser beam was not visible in the water, but it made the objects it struck glow brilliantly, as if self-illuminated.

Many submersibles have mechanical arms and claws. Some of these can rotate well enough to turn a wrench. For geological surveys, submersibles may carry rock drills, corers, and devices to test the sediment on the bottom. For biological study, they can be equipped with "slurp guns" that capture fish and other specimens by sucking them in, or trapdoorlike nets that snap shut around a specimen. This specialized equipment is detachable and can be transferred from one submersible to another. Often, additional equipment is mounted on a removable frame called a

"brow," which is fastened over the bow of the vessel.

The jobs that submersibles do are even more varied than their designs would suggest. They have done everything from pure scientific surveys to recovering the flight recorders from wrecked airliners. In Japan, submersibles have been used to take censuses of food fish in the ocean and in fish farms, and to hunt for the edible seaweed that is an important part of the Japanese diet. In Britain, submersibles have buried cables in the sea floor as deep as 3,000 feet. Off the coast of Turkey, a submersible helped archaeologists investigate a sunken ship wrecked 1,300 years ago. In Hudson's Bay, a submersible repaired a damaged offshore oil well. Off the coast of Georgia, a submersible scooped up samples of ore for a mining company. And in Scotland's Loch Ness, one submersible hunted for the legendary Loch Ness monster, while another towed a forty-foot dummy monster for a movie production.

The first submersibles built in the United States were designed by a Florida newspaper owner named John Perry. Perry's first model, which he built in his garage in 1956, was a small boat made of plastic and plywood. It refused to submerge. From this unsuccessful beginning, he went on to more ambitious and successful submersibles, such as the *Cubmarine* (1962), which can dive to 300 feet. This two-man craft was sold to the United States Army, which used it to recover spent missiles at a testing range in the South Pacific. Larger Perry submersibles include the *PC-8, Deep Diver,* and *Shelf Diver.* The *PC-8* has a transparent plastic nose and a depth capability of 600 feet. It

This Cubmarine *was used in aircraft salvage operations in the Mediterranean Sea.*

has studied garbage-disposal sites in New York Bay, lobster beds in the Gulf of Maine, and coral reefs in the Bahamas. On one assignment, it was flown to the Bering Sea to take part in a study of walrus.

Deep Diver was designed in collaboration with Edwin A. Link. It has a depth capability of over thirteen hundred feet and has a lockout chamber (air lock) for scuba divers. It has been used in training divers and also in biological study projects, as well as by oil companies searching for new, offshore sources of petroleum. It carries a pilot and three passengers.

Shelf Diver, which also carries four persons, has done underwater geological surveys and is now based in Europe. It has also been used experimentally to deliver observers "dry" to an undersea habitat. In one of the most unusual assignments a submersible has ever had, it checked a section of a giant water-supply pipe under the French Alps.

Perry has also developed a series of submersibles for recreation, the *Shark Hunter* and *Reef Hunter*. These are "wet submersibles"; that is, they are open to the water, and the occupants must wear diving gear. Intended as underwater taxis for scuba divers, they are designed for relatively shallow operations, down to about 150 feet, which is about as deep as a prudent amateur diver wants to go.

One of the most newsworthy of submersibles is *Alvin,* which was completed in 1964. Yet *Alvin*'s career did not begin at all spectacularly. Because its support ship was not ready, it spent its first season making shallow dives for the Woods Hole Oceanographic Institution in Massachusetts. The next year was taken up with testing and modification. Finally, in 1966, *Alvin* was pronounced ready for the deepsea work for which it had been designed. Early in that year the little submersible was called out on an emergency mission. A

U.S. hydrogen bomb had been lost in the Mediterranean Sea off the coast of Spain when an air force bomber collided with a tanker plane that was refueling it in mid-air. The bomb lay in almost twenty-five hundred feet of water, separate from the plane, and the bottom was a madman's jumble of steep-sided ravines, abrupt rises, and near-vertical precipices. Had it been an ordinary bomb, the easiest course would have been to leave it there. But it was a twenty-megaton hydrogen bomb, and experts feared that, if it was not recovered, the corrosive seawater would eventually cause it to explode, sending a deadly rain of radiation-laden matter over large parts of Europe and North Africa, and contaminating the sea for many years to come.

Before the bomb could be recovered, it first had to be located. Surface sonar could not pick up an object as small as the bomb,

and the rough terrain of the bottom made it impossible for towed sonar to detect. In addition, the enormous amount of litter on the bottom further confused the sonar response. Therefore the United States Navy, which was handling the mission, decided to use submersibles. Four submersibles took part in the search, the navy's *Deep Jeep,* Perry's *PC-3B, Aluminaut,* and *Alvin.*

The first clue was supplied by a Spanish fisherman near whose boat the bomb had fallen. He told authorities he'd seen half a man in a parachute fall in the water near his boat. This was the bomb with its chute. Using his bearings, *Aluminaut* began searching the bottom with its side-looking sonar. When it detected an object that turned out to be the tail section of the ill-fated B-52 that was carrying the bomb, *Alvin* took up the search, for the fifty-one

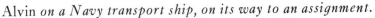
Alvin on a Navy transport ship, on its way to an assignment.

foot *Aluminaut* had difficulty maneuvering along the rugged bottom. *Alvin*'s pilot reasoned that the bomb had probably slid down one of the deep, narrow ravines that seamed the bottom; so he followed the rims of the ravines until he found what appeared to be the track of the bomb. However, he overshot the track, and because of the rough terrain and poor visibility (about thirty feet on an unusually good day) could not find it again for nearly two weeks. After more frustrating near-success, *Alvin* finally located the bomb and its parachute on the mud-covered slope of a ravine, about 2,490 feet down. *Aluminaut* was called in to help surface ships pinpoint the location; then the two submersibles kept watch on the bottom. When *Alvin* had to return to the surface to recharge its batteries, *Aluminaut* was able to remain on station for fourteen hours more. A sonar pinger was dropped next to the bomb to enable the submersibles to locate it quickly.

The next day, *Alvin* took down a lifting cable and tried to anchor it in the mud of the bottom. The attempt failed—because of their nearly neutral buoyancy, small submersibles have very little pushing or pulling power. *Aluminaut* had the power but was not suited for such delicate maneuvering. A few days later (work was interrupted by storms), *Alvin* tried to grab the lines of the bomb's parachute in its mechanical claw. This, too, failed. The navy hastily built a recovery frame hung with grappling hooks and sent it down. *Alvin*'s pilots tried to snag the parachute's lines with the grappling hooks, but tricky bottom currents foiled them. Finally the pilots took another hook from the frame's

anchor line and managed to get it entangled in the chute's lines. The next day the surface support ship began to haul the bomb up, but the line broke, and the bomb was lost again.

It took nine more days of searching before the bomb was once more located, this time about three hundred feet farther down than it had been before. Since the navy was worried that the bomb might slide even farther down in the soft mud, perhaps triggering a landslide that would bury it beyond hope of recovery, *Aluminaut* stood watch over it for twenty-two hours, an impressive performance. Finally the navy sent down an unmanned recovery device named CURV. This was essentially a framework that held a set of motor-powered jaws, plus floodlights and television cameras to guide the five-man surface crew that operated it. CURV managed to get a good grip on the parachute lines, and the whole collection was gingerly reeled in to a depth of 200 feet, where scuba divers fastened additional cables to the bomb for the last stage of the lift. The recovery was a success.

After this strenuous workout, *Alvin* performed a series of dives for the navy near Bermuda, inspecting underwater listening devices and making geological surveys of the bottom. In 1967 it made fifty-five dives. The deepest of these dives was 6,250 feet, the shallowest twenty-six feet. On one dive, a swordfish attacked the submersible, ramming its bill into the fiber-glass outer hull near a viewport. *Alvin* surfaced immediately, carrying the trapped swordfish with it. No major damage was done to the submersible, but the crew were a bit concerned that such attacks might be common.

If the fish had struck the viewport they would have been in trouble. However, other swordfish they later sighted showed no signs of attacking the vessel.

In the fall of 1967 *Alvin* lost its mechanical arm in an accident while preparing to be hoisted aboard the *Lulu,* its mother ship. The sea had become rough, and one of the lines became fouled. Before it could be cut, *Alvin* had collided with *Lulu*'s starboard propeller, breaking the latch that held the mechanical arm to the hull. The arm sank promptly, in 4,500 feet of water. Later, *Alvin* located the missing arm, which was worth over $50,000, and picked it up with a special hook attached under the bow.

Alvin made many more dives, mostly geological and biological studies, using tools developed at Woods Hole. It had a rotary corer for taking rock samples, a gravity corer for sampling mud, sand, and clay, and trapdoor nets for capturing biological specimens. But a launching accident almost put an end to *Alvin*'s career in 1968. *Alvin* was being lowered to the water with two scientists inside and the pilot standing in the open hatch, which was standard operating procedure. Suddenly a support cable broke, and the submersible fell eighteen feet to the water, landing on its side. The men managed to scramble to safety as water poured in through the open hatch, but *Alvin* continued down in 4,920 feet of water.

The next spring, the sunken submersible was located by sonar. A remote-controlled camera was lowered to the site. Its photos showed that *Alvin* was resting upright on the bottom, which would make recovery easier. *Aluminaut* was called in to rescue

its sister submersible. It pulled itself into position over *Alvin*'s open hatch with its mechanical arms, crawling up the side of the smaller craft like a giant bug. This was easier than trying to jockey the fifty-one-foot cylinder into position by its propellers, fighting bottom currents and the tendency of a moving body to keep on moving. Once in place, *Aluminaut* inserted a toggle bar into the hatch of *Alvin,* and the little submersible was hauled up with no difficulty.

Aluminaut, like *Alvin,* was launched in 1964. It can carry a crew of seven: two pilots and five observers. *Aluminaut* was designed for an operating depth of 15,000 feet, but during manufacture flaws were discovered in the metal of its hemispherical end sections. Since the flaws were close to the surface, they could be machined away, but in the process half an inch of metal was removed, reducing the strength of these pieces. As a result, engineers calculated that the safe depth limit was reduced to 8,000 feet. Actually, *Aluminaut*'s deepest dive to date has been 6,250 feet.

More powerful than most submersibles, and able to carry bigger loads of passengers and equipment, *Aluminaut* has been one of the most intensively used deep-submergence research vessels. Even with its reduced depth capability, *Aluminaut* has performed a great deal of very useful work. In addition to its salvage tasks, it discovered and mapped a large bed of scallops miles out to sea off Cape Kennedy, Florida. A valuable scallop fishery business came into being as a result. Near Miami, scientists aboard *Aluminaut* took gravity readings of the bedrock of the Florida Straits, throwing new light on the geological history of North America. On the same dive, they discovered a strong current flowing under the Gulf Stream, in the opposite direction. Although oceanographers had had clues that such a current existed, they thought the evidence was either a temporary phenomenon caused by the tides or else an error in measurement. *Aluminaut* was able to remain on station long enough to make certain that the current was not related to the tide, thus giving positive proof of its existence. Knowledge of this current would be valuable to any submarine commander operating in the area.

For the navy, *Aluminaut* tested new types of sonar which a smaller submersible could not carry. It also retrieved an expensive set of current meters from 3,100 feet down.

Off the coast of Florida and Georgia lies a submarine highland called the Blake Plateau. This plateau is largely covered with a natural pavement of manganese ore. A number of submersibles have explored it, including *Aluminaut,* which brought back a 168-pound chunk of ore in its mechanical claws. Since much of the Blake Plateau is flat, *Aluminaut* was equipped for this trip with a set of wheels, on which it rolled along the bottom like Simon Lake's *Argonaut.*

Deep Quest, built by Lockheed, was launched in 1967, and holds the depth record for American-built submersibles, 8,350 feet. It is relatively large—forty feet long by fifteen feet wide. The twin seven-foot spheres of its pressure hull can carry two pilots and two observers. It carries a great deal of sophisticated electronic and

Deep Quest *rides to a dive location on its specially designed support ship,* Transquest.

The wrecked Navy fighter plane discovered by Deep Quest. *Scuba divers attach extra hoisting cables to lift the plane the last few feet out of the water.*

mechanical equipment. In 1969 *Deep Quest* recovered the "black box" flight recorders from two airliners that had crashed in the Pacific off the Los Angeles International Airport, one from 325 feet and the other from 950 feet. On another occasion, it located the wreck of a World War II fighter plane that had sunk in 3,400 feet of water when its engine failed on a test flight. (The pilot escaped to tell the story.) The plane was far too heavy for *Deep Quest* to lift; so the operator used its mechanical arm to attach a lifting sling to the plane, which was then recovered by a navy ship. Scientists hoped to learn much about the effects of seawater on different metals by studying the plane, which had been under water for more than twenty-six years.

One of *Deep Quest*'s attachments is a Large Object Salvage Module, or LOSM. The LOSM, which divers fasten to the submersible while it is on the surface, is an aluminum frame holding a large pair of mechanical jaws whose edges are lined with ten-inch prongs. With the LOSM, *Deep Quest* can lift loads up to 2,000 pounds. For heavier objects, the submersible can disconnect the LOSM, attach a cable to it, and let it be hauled up by a surface vessel.

In addition to its salvage dives, *Deep Quest* has done geological surveys of submarine canyons off the Southern California coast and has measured the strength of bottom sediments for the navy.

Lockheed has also built two deep submergence rescue vehicles (DSRVs) for the navy. Their function is to rescue the crews of disabled submarines at depths down to 5,000 feet. Their outer hulls are made of fiber-glass-reinforced plastic; their pressure hulls are high-strength steel. The DSRVs, forty-nine feet long and eight feet in diameter, have a crew of three and can take twelve rescuees. A bell-shaped "skirt" beneath the DSRV mates with the hatch of the disabled submarine so that the crew can transfer from one vessel to the other at normal atmospheric pressure without coming in contact with the water. The DSRVs, ready for use at twenty-four hours' notice, can be transported on a truck, or the deck of a ship, or carried piggyback by a nuclear attack sub-marine. They can also be flown on a large transport plane.

The idea of the DSRV was born after the *Thresher* disaster, and the navy originally planned to have a fleet of twelve. However, the Vietnam War devoured the money that the government had allocated for DSRVs, and the program was cut off at two rescue vessels.

One unusual submersible was the *Ben Franklin*, designed by Jacques Piccard

A DSRV looms eerily in the water as a frogman gives it a visual inspection.

The Ben Franklin *rests on a dock in Florida.*

and built in Switzerland for the Grumman Aircraft Corporation in 1967. The *Ben Franklin* is a mesoscaph (Greek for "middle boat"), a vessel designed mainly for free drifting at depths down to about two thousand feet. The *Ben Franklin*'s elaborately equipped, forty-eight-foot hull can hold five persons for up to forty-five days, which makes unusually long observation voyages possible.

In the summer of 1969, Piccard and four scientists took the *Ben Franklin* on a 1,440-mile voyage in the Gulf Stream. The voyage made no headlines, for nothing sensational happened. The scientists were disappointed at finding very little marine life in the clear, blue waters of the Gulf Stream, but they learned valuable new information about the way the great current threw off eddies and was fed by tributary currents. Once a powerful eddy threw the *Ben Franklin* so far out of the Gulf Stream that it had to radio its support ship to tow it back. They also discovered the existence of invisible waves within the Gulf Stream when their vessel was suddenly tossed violently up and down. They measured wave heights up to 300 feet—vital information for submarine commanders to be aware of. Such waves may be responsible for a number of unexplained submarine sinkings.

As the current carried the *Ben Franklin* along, Piccard and his associates took many measurements of the speed, temperature, pressure, density, and salinity of the water. They also carried out a series of experiments on how a long confinement affects the health and disposition of the inmates of a submersible. They found out that their elaborate germ-proofing operations seemed to have little effect, for all the crew came down with colds.

After the Gulf Stream study, the *Ben Franklin* investigated what happened to industrial waste dumped off the coast of New Jersey. This assignment was followed by rock sampling off southern Florida, using a mechanical arm borrowed from *Alvin*. In 1970 the *Ben Franklin* was badly damaged by being slammed into a coral reef when its mother ship's mooring broke.

Asherah is a seventeen-foot, two-man craft built by General Dynamics for the University of Pennsylvania, chiefly for archaeological research. In 1967 *Asherah* took a series of stereo photographs of the 1,300-year-old shipwreck mentioned earlier in this chapter, completing in one hour a task that would have taken a team of archaeologist-divers several months. *Asherah* has also done geological studies for the Smithsonian Institution and studied fish for the United States government and for universities.

General Dynamics also built a series of small submersibles named *Star. Star I,* the first submersible to be powered by a fuel cell, was used in experimental work by the navy. It is now on exhibition in the Philadelphia Maritime Museum. *Star II* is a battery-powered survey vessel with a depth capability of 1,200 feet. *Star III* is a workboat with an operating depth of 2,000 feet. Its mechanical arm has interchangeable hands for different types of work. It was donated to the Scripps Institution of Oceanography in California and is now in storage. *Sea Cliff* and *Turtle,* also General Dynamics boats, are patterned after the *Alvin.* Built for the navy, they were intended to work on an underwater test range off the Bahamas, recovering spent torpedoes and missiles and inspecting underwater tracking instruments. Eventually they were assigned instead to the navy base at San Diego, California.

Nekton is the name of a series of submersibles built by General Oceanographics, a California firm. The *Nekton*s have inspected offshore oil wells, surveyed the disastrous underwater oil-well leaks at Santa Barbara, California, and surveyed the Straits of Gibraltar for laying a natural-gas pipeline from Africa to Europe. They have also done survey dives in the Great Lakes, inspected the deep-water sewer outlet of the city of Los Angeles, observed the effects of radiation waste on marine life, and studied the formation of coral reefs in the Caribbean. On one assignment, a *Nekton* submersible directed the placement of a huge sewer outlet pipe in Canada, phoning instructions to the crane and barge crews on the surface 220 feet above. A dramatic assignment came when *Deep Quest* became fouled in a cable 432 feet down. A *Nekton* came to the rescue, cutting the cable with its mechanical claw and freeing the trapped submersible.

Archimède is a submersible built by the French Navy for very deep dives. Heavily constructed and very slow, it is as much a bathyscaphe as a submersible. With a maximum depth rated at 36,000 feet, it has dived as deep as 31,600 feet in the Pacific. As early as 1962 it set a record by diving to 28,000 feet near Japan. It has also explored the Puerto Rico Trench for the United States Navy, diving to 25,000 feet.

Argyronète is another advanced French submersible. Eighty-two feet long and equipped with diesel engines for surface cruising, it seems more like a regular submarine than a research submersible. Actually, it is equipped to function as a self-propelled undersea habitat, and ten people can live in it for as long as ten days. It is designed primarily to serve as a base for divers on deep-water oil projects.

The United States Navy's *NR-1* was launched in January 1969. Because of strict navy secrecy, little is known about its operating capabilities. It is 140 feet long, 12 feet wide, and 25 feet high, and it can cruise submerged for many days at better than five miles per hour. So far as is known, it is the only nuclear-powered research submersible in the world. It carries a crew of five, plus two scientist-observers, and its life-support system can keep them functioning for forty-five days. Missions planned for *NR-1* by the navy include investigating wrecked ships and aircraft, assisting in rescue and recovery operations, doing oceanographic and geological re-

search, searching for mineral resources, and studying fish and shellfish that are eaten or otherwise used by man.

Not exactly submersibles but closely related are the Scripps Institute's FLIP and a number of undersea bulldozers built in Japan and Britain.

FLIP, for FLoating Instrument Platform, is a pencil-shaped vessel 355 feet long. Technically, it is known as a spar buoy. It is towed to its observation site; then ballast tanks in the stern section are flooded, so that the whole vessel "flips" slowly into an upright position, with the stern as much as 300 feet below the water. In this position, it is amazingly stable. Even in a severe storm, it bobs up and down only a foot or so, and it rolls very little. Most of the work space is above water, but there is also an underwater lab compartment. FLIP is specially designed for investigating the behavior of sound waves underwater.

In 1969 the Japanese firm of Hitachi,

FLIP, a floating observation platform for oceanographic work, can be lowered to horizontal position and towed like a ship.

best known in the United States for electronic products, sold an underwater bulldozer to a contractor building a fish farm. The machine, working down as far as sixty feet, was remotely controlled by an operator on a surface vessel. Two weeks later, a second Japanese firm announced it would produce underwater bulldozers. In 1970 another Japanese underwater bulldozer appeared on the market, this time controlled by a diver and with a working depth of ninety feet. Britain has a four-wheeled vehicle called the *Seabed Crawler,* which began shallow-water mining operations on the continental shelf in 1970.

In the United States in the early 1970s, most work with submersibles was being carried on by the navy using its own vessels. Many privately owned submersibles had been put in mothballs for lack of funds, since the navy had been their chief customer. Most of those that were still working were small boats, like the Perry boats and the *Nekton*s. One reason may be that the small submersibles are so much cheaper to operate than the large ones, and they can do many jobs just as well.

The biggest project planned for the early 1970s is FAMOUS (French-American Mid-Ocean Undersea Study), which will explore the Mid-Atlantic Rift. This is a rugged undersea chasm that splits the crest of the great Mid-Atlantic Ridge, a mountain chain that snakes across the Atlantic floor. The French *Archimède,* already mentioned, will take part, as will the *SP-3000,* Cousteau's deep-ranging successor to *Deepstar-4000. SP-3000* can descend to 3,000 meters, or nearly 10,000 feet. *Alvin,* equipped with a new titanium hull

that will allow it to dive to 12,000 feet, will be the American participant.

The Mid-Atlantic Ridge and Rift were discovered in the 1950s, by an American oceanographic expedition. Up to now it is known only through observations taken from surface ships. The direct observations made by these submersibles, penetrating into the deepest parts of the rift, should provide information of tremendous value to geologists and to everyone interested in the story of the earth's formation.

Kuroshio II, a Japanese research submersible, has dived to 650 feet. Power comes via electric cable from a support ship.

11

Habitats

BACK in the 1950s a navy doctor, Captain George Bond, was thinking about the inordinate amount of time a diver had to spend in decompression after each dive. It could happen—and sometimes did—that a diver working very deep spent fifteen minutes at work and the rest of the day decompressing. Bond thought this was very wasteful, as had many men before him who had been involved with diving.

Experiments had shown that once a diver reached a given depth and stayed there for a certain time, the gases dissolved in his body reached the saturation point; that is, his body had absorbed all the gases it could absorb at that particular pressure. After this point was reached, the time needed for decompression would not increase, no matter how long the diver stayed down. But, in actuality, the cold of the water and the stress of working under high pressure tired the diver out quickly, so that

he needed to return to the surface. The deeper he went, the fewer minutes he could stay on the bottom. This was as true for scuba divers as for helmeted divers.

This being the case, Bond reasoned, if there were some way of providing the diver with a place *under the water* where he could rest and warm up between dives, *at the same pressure as that of his working level,* most of his time could be used for productive work instead of being spent in decompression procedures. If a suitable shelter could be built, divers could even spend several days underwater, not returning to the surface until their jobs were completed. Bond called this idea *saturation diving,* and the proposed undersea living quarters he called a *habitat.*

In 1957 Bond proposed his idea to his navy superiors, but they were not at all enthusiastic. However, the idea was picked up by Cousteau, who was an old

SEALAB I, the first U.S. underwater habitat. In its cigar-shaped hull, four men spent two weeks at a depth of 193 feet.

acquaintance of Bond's and familiar with his work. Cousteau, too, was interested in finding a way to enable divers to stay down longer. He had had a great deal of trouble doing oceanographic work from the surface. For example, towing cables and power lines persistently got tangled or snapped off. He was convinced that divers could do the job better if only they could remain underwater long enough.

Another person interested in the same goal was Edwin A. Link, an inventor, industrialist, and long-time enthusiast of underwater exploration. Born in Binghamton, New York, in 1904, Link became a licensed airplane pilot in 1926. In 1929,

when he was twenty-five years old, he invented the Link Trainer, a device in which hundreds of thousands of pilots have learned the basic skills of flying without leaving the ground. In 1959 he retired from business to devote himself full time to underwater research and archaeology.

In 1962 Cousteau and Link independently gave saturation diving and habitats their first tests. Cousteau set up a habitat in the Mediterranean near the great port of Marseilles. He named the experiment *Conshelf-I,* for the continental shelf on which the habitat rested. Here, thirty-three feet below the surface, two divers were to spend a week. The habitat, a seventeen-by-eight-foot steel cylinder, was linked to the surface by telephone. Electric power and other needs were supplied by power lines and pipelines from a surface support ship. This became standard procedure for habitats, for it would be impractical to have an electric power plant on the sea floor, and batteries would wear out too quickly.

During their stay below, the *Conshelf-I* divers performed a number of experiments and observations, diving down to eighty-five feet on some assignments. This, of course, was nothing for a trained scuba diver, but Cousteau was not trying to set any records. His aim was to see how well human beings could adapt to living underwater.

After spending a week at twice normal atmospheric pressure, the divers showed no ill effects at all. Encouraged by the results of this project, Cousteau planned a series of similar habitats, each one located deeper than the one before.

Link's experiment also was carried out

in the Mediterranean off the coast of France. He picked the Bay of Villefranche for his site. Here the depth of the water was varied enough for all the trials Link wanted to carry out. Villefranche was also home port for the U.S. Sixth Fleet, which he could count on for help in an emergency.

Link's plan was to send a diver down to 200 feet for twenty-four hours or more, trying for depth where Cousteau had tried for time. For a habitat, he used an upright cylindrical diving chamber equipped with an air lock, a seat, and a desk-level shelf on which the diver could rest his head for a nap, spread out his meals, or write reports. The chamber was also designed to serve as a decompression chamber following the dive. Because of the depth, the diver had to breathe a helium-oxygen mixture to avoid nitrogen narcosis. The breathing mixture was supplied through a hose from the support ship. Link tested the chamber himself at shallow depths before turning it over to the diver he had chosen, a twenty-nine-year-old Belgian named Robert Stenuit.

On the day of the big dive, the chamber, filled with the helium-oxygen mixture, was lowered over the side. Stenuit dived into the water and swam in through the air lock. After a practice period to get acclimated to the helium mixture, which he had never used before, Stenuit winched himself gradually down to the 200-foot level. He left the chamber several times for brief dives with a scuba rig, but each time the cold of the water forced him to return quickly. As you remember, a diver's body loses heat much more rapidly in helium than in ordinary air.

An additional problem with helium turned out to be equally serious. Sound travels three times faster in helium than it does in normal air, so that both the pitch and the rate of speech are raised. A man who normally speaks in a deep voice becomes a soprano in a helium atmosphere. His words become unclear, and he sounds like Donald Duck or the chattering chipmunks in animal cartoons. The effect is like playing a 33-r.p.m. phonograph record at 78 r.p.m., only more so.

This characteristic of helium had been known since the United States Navy began using helium breathing mixtures back in the 1920s, but divers' helmet telephones worked so badly at that time that it was just one more inconvenience. But for the Link crew it was not just an inconvenience. It nearly wrecked the experiment, for the people on the surface could not understand a word Stenuit said. They could not even tell whether he was saying yes or no. In the end, Stenuit had to send messages in Morse code.

The problem of helium's distorting effect on speech still plagues the users of habitats. No solution for it has yet been found. Men in habitats are sometimes able to make themselves understood by speaking very slowly and deliberately. Sometimes they must write messages to each other instead and communicate with the surface by Morse code. Several companies have developed electronic devices to convert the squeaky, chattering voices of helium-breathing aquanauts back into something like normal speech, but as of the early 1970s these converters have not come into general use.

Aside from the difficulty with communication, the Link experiment went well for the first twenty hours. Then a chain of accidents happened. Just as Stenuit informed Link in Morse code that he felt fine and would like to stay down another day, it was discovered that leaks in the breathing system had let most of the helium escape. Link sent a crew ashore in the ship's launch to get a new supply of helium. As they returned, loaded down with over a ton of helium cylinders, a strong wind swooped down on the bay. The launch, heavily laden at the stern, shipped water and sank. The men swam easily to safety, but Link had to think very quickly about what to do with Stenuit.

There was enough helium left in the cylinder to last through the decompression period if Stenuit was brought up immediately. However, the sea was too rough for this, so they had to begin decompression with the cylinder under water. About noon the surface crew began to raise Stenuit, lowering the pressure in his cylinder by stages, but the sea did not calm down enough to bring him on deck until evening. Once there, the cylinder was laid down on its side so that Stenuit could at last stretch out.

By Link's calculations (the standard decompression tables did not cover such a long submersion) he would need a total of fifty-four hours' decompression time. Part of this, of course, he had already gone through while still in the water. But as the pressure eased down, Stenuit felt sharp pains in his wrist—the beginning of an attack of the bends. Pressure in the cylinder had to be raised again, and Stenuit had to spend sixty hours in his cramped container, being fed through the air lock.

Despite this setback, the results of the experiment were positive. Stenuit reported that he felt no discomfort at all in the high-pressure helium atmosphere. This was a go-ahead signal to future experiments with long, deep dives. The major problems were found to be the difficulty of communication caused by the effect of the helium, and the cold. Little could be done about the first except to equip habitats with a Morse code sender, but the second could be solved by better-insulated suits or electrically heated suits for the diver. As a follow-up, Link used his diving cylinder to recover the sunken launch plus some of the helium tanks from 240 feet of water.

Cousteau's second habitat experiment, *Conshelf-II*, took place in 1963. For the site, he picked a coral reef called Sha'ab Rumi (Arabic for "Roman Reef"), on the desolate African coast of the Red Sea. Cousteau chose this searingly hot, out-of-the-way location because of its wretched climate and because it was so hard to reach. An experimenter here was really on his own. If he could manage a habitat here, Cousteau later wrote, he could do it anywhere.

Conshelf-II was a much larger-scale experiment than *Conshelf-I*. The habitat, dubbed "Starfish House" because of its shape, was to shelter five divers for a month, thirty-six feet down. Two divers were to spend a week in a separate, two-man "Deep Cabin" at ninety feet. There was also an underwater hangar for the diving saucer *DS-2*, which was used for observation dives down to 1,000 feet.

In addition to testing man's physical ability to stand longer and deeper dives, Cousteau wanted to learn whether habitat-based divers could successfully perform work under the sea. A regular schedule of tasks was laid out, which the aquanauts performed successfully. They also made extensive biological studies, discovering a new species of sea urchin with a radarlike scanning organ on top of its spiny shell, and an odd-looking crab that spent its time bulldozing shelters out of sand and coral fragments. They captured fish and sent them to the surface in plastic bags, to be shipped alive to the Oceanographic Institute of Monaco.

Sharks were an ever-present menace, so the men, working underwater, built a metal "shark cage" where they could take refuge. Another problem was swarms of bloodthirsty "sea mosquitoes," small, fast-moving crustaceans that attacked every part of a diver's body not protected by his mask or suit, drawing blood with their sharp mouth parts. The men could escape the sharks by going into the shark cage, but there was no way of escaping the sea mosquitoes outside of returning to the habitat.

The divers in the main habitat, thirty-six feet down, were comfortable throughout their stay—in fact, a good deal more comfortable than Cousteau and the rest of the topside crew. But the divers at the ninety-foot level did not fare so well. They lost their appetites and did not want to eat or drink. One developed an earache and had trouble sleeping. This did not, however, keep them from going out on their diving missions. Most of the missions were carried out at 165 feet, but on the sixth day Cousteau asked them to go to 330 feet. They actually pushed on to 363 feet, but did not tell their chief till later. The pur-

pose of the deep dive had been to learn whether helium had a narcotic effect at that depth. The dive proved it was safe.

For his third *Conshelf* project, in 1965, Cousteau returned to the Mediterranean, this time 328 feet below the surface. The habitat designed for *Conshelf-III* was an eighteen-foot sphere divided into two stories. The lower level was for sleeping, diving, and toilets, the upper level for meals, communications, and data gathering. Five men would spend two weeks here, working on a simulated oil-well head. Their mission was to test the possibility of using divers to man offshore oil wells, instead of relying on offshore towers, which are vulnerable to storms and collisions by ships.

To conserve the scarce and expensive helium in their breathing mixtures, the divers used a closed-circuit system, breathing the same atmosphere over and over. This is now standard procedure for all habitats using helium. In such a system, the atmosphere must be continually purified, and oxygen added to replace what the divers use up. In *Conshelf-III* the used air was filtered through a cryogenerator—an ultracold freezing unit—which froze out carbon dioxide and other impurities.

While working outside the habitat, each diver was supplied with "heliox," as Cousteau called the mixture, through a hose from the habitat. Even so, each diver wore an aqualung charged with the same mixture, as a safety measure in case the pump that supplied him broke down.

Cousteau wished to make the habitat as independent of surface support as possible. The aquanauts had to prepare all their own meals, using an electric stove since the heliox mixture would not support combustion. If one of them struck a match, it fizzled out. Cigarettes would not stay lit. Water would not boil, even when heated far above the normal boiling point.

The food supply was kept cold by the cryogenerator. Fresh water for washing—nine tons of it—was stored outside the habitat in a giant balloon. The gases for the breathing mixture were stored in the habitat. The only connections with the surface were the vital electric power and communication lines. But the aquanauts were not isolated. Every day Cousteau visited them in a diving saucer, and a closed-circuit TV camera kept constant watch over them inside their giant sphere. Communication was aided by an electric facsimile machine; the aquanauts would write messages on its sender and it would reproduce them at the other end.

The artificial wellhead on which they were to work was set up at 370 feet of depth, about half a football field's length away from the habitat, since it had to be within reach of the breathing hoses. For protection against the cold, the divers wore two foam-rubber suits, one over the other. Even so, the suits provided little warmth, since the pressure of the water crushed them flat, destroying the insulating power of their tiny air pockets. So Cousteau equipped each diver with a special insulating vest, made of microscopic bubbles of incompressible ebonite (the hard rubber used in combs) embedded in soft rubber. Even with this added protection, the helium breathing mixture robbed the divers of heat so fast that they could not work outside for more than about an hour without severe discom-

fort. After that, they had to go into the habitat to warm up with the aid of special infrared heaters.

There were some tense moments while the five-ton "Christmas tree" wellhead assembly was lowered to the sea floor from a barge on the surface. Eight-foot waves caused the barge to rock violently, and the big assembly of pipes and valves danced up and down like a giant yo-yo. Divers and diving saucer scattered for safety until the wellhead was safely planted on the bottom. Once it was in place, the divers performed various repair and maintenance jobs on it with surprising efficiency. Oil-field engineers watching the work from the surface via closed-circuit TV were amazed when the five-man team removed and replaced a 400-pound valve in forty-five minutes—half the time it would have required on land. The valve was easier to handle in the water, since the water's buoyancy cut its weight by a half.

Bad weather was a continuous problem from the start, even threatening at one point to rip loose the electric power lines. Most of the time it made the water too muddy for photography or biological studies. Cousteau asked his men if they would stay on for another week to complete some planned experiments. They agreed, and they were willing to stay on even longer. Toward the end of the third week, however, they were clearly becoming exhausted, so Cousteau called a halt. The big sphere dropped its ballast and floated to the surface. The men spent three and one half days decompressing. When they emerged from the habitat they were greeted as heroes and shown on TV all over Europe. Cousteau was now ready to have divers live even deeper. His eventual goal was to have them live at 666 feet and dive as deep as 1,300 feet. Within this range lay the resources of every part of the world's continental shelves.

While Cousteau was busy with his *Conshelf* projects, the United States Navy decided to conduct its own experiments with habitats. The first program, SEALAB I, was carried out in 1964 under the leadership of Dr. Bond. The site chosen for the project was an underwater plateau near Bermuda, where four aquanauts were to spend about two weeks at 200 feet. Actually, the habitat stood at 193 feet, but the difference was not considered significant.

The navy gave its aquanauts thorough training. Before SEALAB I was given final approval, three of the divers had spent an equivalent amount of time in a pressure tank, at a simulated pressure of 200 feet of water, breathing a helium-nitrogen-oxygen mixture like the one they would use in the sea. The habitat itself was a steel chamber forty feet long by ten feet in diameter. It looked like a fat cigar. It was an experimental model, and facts learned during this experiment would be used to design better habitats.

The aquanauts carried out such projects as placing sonar beacons on the sea floor, installing current meters, and setting up lights for nighttime photography. They also tested a shark-attraction system devised by the navy, but it failed to draw any sharks.

The submersible *Star I* was involved in the project. The aquanauts were asked to check on its operation and assist it in landing on a dummy submarine hatch. During this task, the scuba regulator of one aquanaut failed, causing him to breathe his own exhalations. He collapsed from carbon-dioxide poisoning at the entrance to the habitat. Fortunately, a teammate reached him in time, dragged him inside, and revived him.

Food, newspapers, and magazines were sent down daily to the habitat in a sealed pressure container, and the men were adjusting well to their artificial undersea environment, although the habitat became uncomfortably damp. But navy meteorologists reported a hurricane was on its way up from the Caribbean, and project supervisors decided to bring up men and habitat on the eleventh day, while they still had time to get out of the way of the storm.

Although the approaching hurricane cut short the planned experiments, the navy was highly satisfied. SEALAB I had now also proved what Cousteau and Link had already demonstrated: that men could live and work for extended periods of time at depths that a few years earlier had been considered prohibitive.

SEALAB II followed in 1965. It was a much more ambitious project than SEALAB I, involving more men and more difficult conditions. The location for the habitat was a ledge on the side of a submarine canyon off La Jolla, California. This location was chosen so that the aquanauts could make deep experimental dives without having to go dangerously far from the habitat. In addition, the navy wanted to study the way men reacted to a prolonged stay in a cold, dark environment.

Three teams of ten men each were to spend fifteen-day shifts on the bottom. Two men were to stay down for thirty days. One of these two was the former

SEALAB II ready to be towed to its site off La Jolla, California.

astronaut Scott Carpenter. A career navy man, Carpenter felt that the exploration of the "inner space" of the ocean depths offered even more of a challenge than the exploration of outer space.

Before the experiment started, the aquanauts were put through a special six-month training course. They were given cram courses in physics and physiology so that they would understand the deep-water pressure that would be affecting them and their materials. They became thoroughly familiar with the workings of their scuba apparatus, and they learned how to communicate with each other while out on a dive, both important for safety.

The SEALAB II habitat was a fifty-seven-foot cylinder with a "conning tower," which was actually a ballast tank, on top. It looked like a railroad tank car without wheels, but inside it was as comfortable as the navy's designers could make it. Everything possible had been done to

overcome the problems that had bothered the aquanauts of SEALAB I. For instance, cold had been a problem in SEALAB I, as in all deep-water habitats, because of the helium atmosphere. So the floors of SEALAB II had heating cables embedded in them, warming the whole inside of the habitat. An elaborate surface support system was provided, complete with round-the-clock monitoring by closed-circuit TV. In this way, even if the aquanauts were struck by some disaster and unable to call for help, the topside crew could immediately rush aid to them.

The ledge where SEALAB II perched was 205 feet down. It was not level, so the habitat came to rest at a noticeable angle. The aquanauts promptly nicknamed their out-of-line underwater residence the "Tiltin' Hilton," after the well-known chain of hotels. The tilt became annoying after a while, although it did not prevent

SEALAB II aquanauts check the habitat's connections as it begins to sink to the sea floor.

the aquanauts from carrying out their jobs.

These jobs included setting up various underwater structures, testing underwater tools, and setting up an underwater "weather station" along with a small army of instruments for testing the water. There were also the daily chores of housekeeping and maintaining the equipment in good shape.

Before and after each dive the aquanauts were given tests of strength and manual dexterity just outside the habitat. Each evening they had to fill out checklists of their activities and moods during the day. Now and then they were given arith-

Tuffy, a dolphin trained by Navy scientists, carries out his assigned task in a successful underwater experiment.

metic tests and "brainteasers" to see how well their minds were functioning. In addition, every day they sent samples of their breath, blood, urine, and saliva to the topside medical men. The divers on SEA-LAB II were probably the most thoroughly studied divers in history.

One of the work projects involved a dolphin named Tuffy, who had been trained to respond to sound signals, bring tools to the divers, and rescue them in case they lost their bearings in the dark, muddy water. In one experiment, Tuffy brought a guideline from the habitat to a diver who signaled that he was in distress. Tuffy also carried mail from topside to the aquanauts in a waterproof pouch.

The men also tested electrically heated wet suits, some powered by a battery belt around the aquanaut's waist, some powered by an electric line from the habitat. The suits enabled the aquanauts to stay out for as long as two hours—about twice the usual length of a working dive without heated suits.

On the first day of the experiment, Carpenter spoke from the sea floor to his fellow astronaut Gordon Cooper, at that moment in orbit around the earth. The conversation was carried by phone from the habitat to the surface, then transmitted by radio to Cooper in his capsule high above the earth. Carpenter's helium-distorted voice was hard to understand, but the fact that the message had been transmitted at all was quite an accomplishment. Later in the experiment, SEALAB divers spoke via the same sort of hookup to Cousteau's team in *Conshelf-III,* halfway around the world and even deeper underwater than SEALAB II. It was hoped

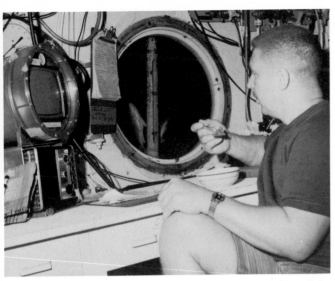

Oceanographer Arthur Fleggsig studies fish outside the viewport of SEALAB II. Tube outside port is a water thermometer.

that some day scientists working simultaneously on different underwater projects could exchange information this way.

Thanks to Dr. Bond's excellent medical supervision, there were only two casualties among the SEALAB II divers. One was an aquanaut who suffered a slight case of the bends. The other was Carpenter, who was badly poisoned by a sculpin. The sculpin is an ugly bottom-dwelling fish with poisonous spines. For some reason, large numbers of sculpins were attracted to the habitat, clustering around it like holiday crowds at the beach. During one assignment that demanded all his attention, Carpenter accidentally swung his hand against a sculpin's spine. Within a few minutes he was suffering excruciating pain. His hand and arm swelled up to several times normal size. He choked up and could barely breathe. The project doctors wanted to pull him up and send him to a

hospital for treatment, but Carpenter asked to be allowed to stay with the project. The doctors reluctantly agreed and sent down drugs to treat him. Twenty-four hours later, Carpenter had recovered completely.

SEALAB II was given tremendous publicity. The navy, delighted with its success, determined to follow it up with a third SEALAB, this time at a depth of 620 feet. The site, off the southern California coast, was surveyed beforehand by the submersible *Deepstar-4000* to make sure that it was suitable. The habitat was to float just above the ocean floor, tethered to anchor weights by cables which were made adjustable to avoid the annoying tilt of SEALAB II. Carpenter was to supervise the project, this time from the surface,

Aquanauts assemble an underwater structure as part of their training program for SEALAB III.

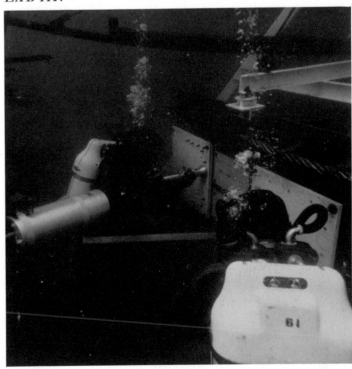

for he was suffering from a bone disease that attacks people who work under high pressure.

Unfortunately, SEALAB III seemed to be jinxed from the beginning. Its cost ran $3,000,000 over the original estimate. The project was far behind schedule. The divers were not given sufficient training for the depth at which they were to work. And sloppy workmanship, which at that point was plaguing so many government projects—the *Apollo* disaster was one—also struck the habitat. The neoprene sleeves through which the various power, gas, and water lines entered the hull were not quite the right size, and they were not put in correctly. It was a small defect, and one which unwary inspectors on the surface did not catch, but it proved to be fatal.

When the habitat was lowered, the costly helium breathing mixture began to disappear at an alarming rate. A team of aquanauts sent down to investigate the trouble reported that the helium was leaking out through the badly fitting neoprene sleeves. The navy command considered postponing the project for repairs, but the men, anxious to save it, volunteered to go down and repair the damage on the spot. While doing this work, a civilian aquanaut named Berry Cannon, a veteran of SEALAB II, went into convulsions and collapsed. Two teammates took turns massaging his heart as he was rushed to the surface in a pressurized personnel delivery chamber, but he died without regaining consciousness.

An investigation showed that the carbon-dioxide filter was missing from the scuba rig he had been using. The effect of breathing his own waste gases at 600 feet

was quickly fatal to Cannon. Why such a careless accident should have been allowed to claim the life of a man was never learned. But a navy inquiry found that the divers had been awake for twenty hours before the fatal dive, and that they had been given amphetamine "pep pills." The divers were tired, under emotional strain, and affected by artificial stimulants. Thus, their minds may not have been functioning clearly, and Cannon apparently neglected to check his breathing gear properly before putting it on.

The habitat was pulled up and sent to a shipyard for repairs while the navy reconsidered the whole program. Eventually the SEALAB III program was discontinued and the funds were spent for other purposes.

SEALAB III was designed to withstand depths of over 600 feet. Bad workmanship caused it to fail, and the project was cancelled.

While SEALAB III was beset with difficulties, another, far less elaborate, habitat was functioning beautifully on the floor of the Caribbean, off the Virgin Islands. This project was TEKTITE I, run jointly by the navy, NASA, and the department of the interior. Four civilian scientists spent sixty days living at a depth of fifty feet, studying marine life and the geology of the sea floor. One of their major projects was studying the spiny lobster, the chief commercial source of lobster tails. The spiny-lobster population of the Virgin Islands had been declining, and it was hoped that these studies would point to a way to restore their numbers. To identify the lobsters they were observing, the men tagged them with color-coded tabs. Some lobsters were tagged with tiny, beeping sonar transmitters so that the scientists could track them at night, when spiny lobsters go out to hunt.

Since TEKTITE I was located at a relatively shallow depth, the aquanauts did not need to breathe a helium mixture. However, to avoid the risk of oxygen poisoning, they breathed a mixture of 91 percent nitrogen and 9 percent oxygen.

The men were kept isolated from other human beings, communicating with the surface only by telephone, for one of the most important goals of the project was to learn how scientists would behave in isolation. NASA needed this information in order to plan orbiting, manned space stations, where the astronauts would be equally isolated. The results were encouraging, and information gained from TEKTITE was

Artist's conception of the very successful TEKTITE habitat. Cage around entrance hatch protects divers from sharks.

used in planning the SKYLAB project, in which teams of spacemen were to remain in orbit for as long as 56 days.

When the project was finished, the habitat was left in place and used for a follow-up, TEKTITE II, in which a number of five-man teams took part for two weeks each. One team was all female; they were the first women aquanauts.

TEKTITE II continued the biological studies begun on TEKTITE I, with particular emphasis on the lobster project and the ecology of coral reefs. One team experimented with the effects of different pollutants on coral. They learned that four commonly used insect killers, even in extremely small trace amounts, could be fatal to the coral. Another team concentrated on the sounds which some species of coral-reef fish use to communicate with each other. If these sound signals, some of them very faint, could be identified, they could be used in fish farming. Feeding signals could be broadcast to lure food fish into pens, while warning signals would repel predators. This is still a long way off, but it is typical of the kind of research oceanographers are doing with an eye to feeding an overpopulated world.

The women's team, four biologists and an engineer, studied such things as the escape reactions of fish when threatened by predators, marine plants (they recorded 153 different species, including 26 never before reported from the area), and the different rates at which small plants and animals grew on natural sea grass and artificial plastic grass. The last experiment had a very practical purpose. If algae could be made to grow on artificial sea grass, it would be able to support a food chain that could be used in fish farming. They found that the plastic grass worked as well as the real grass, and the idea is now being used in some fish farms.

The psychological studies begun on TEKTITE I were also continued, with topside observers watching the aquanauts over TV. One interesting discovery was that the more religious a person was, the less well he performed in isolation. Scientists who had been sickly as children adapted better than those who had been healthy. A person who had been either an only child or the oldest child in the family also adapted well. These findings upset a number of opinions that psychologists had cherished for years.

Edwin Link had also continued his experiments with habitats. In 1964 he sent Stenuit and Jon Lindbergh, son of the famed aviator Charles Lindbergh, down to 432 feet for two days. The habitat Link had designed for this project, which took place in the Bahamas, was quite unconventional. Instead of the heavy steel cylinders and spheres used for other habitats, it was an eight-by-four-foot rubber tent, kept inflated with helium breathing mixture. He called it the SPID, for Submersible, Portable, Inflatable Dwelling.

Stenuit and Lindbergh made some shakedown dives with the SPID before the big dive. With this preparation, they were lowered to the bottom in a decompression chamber. Plans had called for a depth of 400 feet; they ended up thirty-two feet lower, under an extra atmosphere of pressure. They slid out of the cylinder-shaped decompression chamber and swam to the SPID. Immediately, things began to go wrong.

Lindbergh hooked up the electrical connections with the surface and turned on the light in the underwater tent. The light bulb burned for five seconds and went out. Working by flashlight, they plugged in the radiator. It refused to work. Worst of all, the container holding their air purifier had flooded on the way down, and the machine was unusable. Stenuit wrestled the spare air filter in from outside. They could not get the lid off the four-foot cylinder. There should have been a valve in the lid to equalize the pressure, for the filter had been sealed into its container at atmospheric pressure, and the pressure in the SPID was nearly two hundred pounds per square inch. But someone on the surface had put on the wrong lid. There was no equalizing valve. The lid was clamped tight on the container by a force of about four tons. The men could not budge it.

Without light or heat, and with the carbon-dioxide content in the habitat rising dangerously, the two divers retreated to the decompression cylinder, which had been kept standing by in case of an emergency. In Morse code they informed the surface crew of their predicament. Link hauled up the flooded air filter, fixed it, and sent it down again. The two men dragged it into the SPID, got it open, and plugged it in. To their relief, the motor began purring just in time.

Stenuit and Lindbergh made a number of dives to explore the bottom. They had to stay close to the SPID, since their breathing supply came through fifty-foot hoses. At that depth, an aqualung cylinder would have been used up in a few minutes. They wore special wet suits composed of little air cells, which they kept inflated with compressed air. The trapped air provided fairly good insulation. Once Lindbergh had fixed the radiator, the two men were comfortable in the SPID. They were ready to stay down for a week, watching the fascinating pageant of marine life just outside their habitat. But Link, not wishing to take unnecessary chances, brought them up on schedule, after forty-eight hours. Decompression time was ninety-two hours—the men would have needed no more time if they had stayed down for six months.

In 1972 the NOAA (National Oceanic and Atmospheric Administration) ran a three-month project named FLARE off southern Florida. Seven teams of scientists took part, including an all-woman team headed by the chief woman diver from TEKTITE II. The teams were limited to three by the small size of the habitat, a steel tank measuring only ten by eight feet inside. Designed by engineering students at the University of New Hampshire, the habitat was named EDALHAB. Easily portable, it was shuttled among four sites, all at a depth of forty-five feet. At this depth, the divers were able to breathe ordinary air.

The main mission of the project was to study the ecology of coral reefs. In one study, the divers examined a reef near the sewage outlet of the city of Miami. They found that the reef was dying. The clouds of sediment in the water cut off the sunlight, so that the green algae that live in a healthy coral reef could not thrive. Deprived of the oxygen they normally got from the algae, the coral polyps could not survive long. The scientists believed that the sewage, polluted and filthy as it was,

The Perry Hydro-Lab, *a shallow-water habitat, has housed scientists, sport divers, and even movie-making crews.*

was not the chief cause of the deadly blanket of dirt in the water. Major culprits, they believed, were runoff from construction sites on land and clouds of sediment stirred up by dredging.

In a study with more hopeful results, a FLARE team built an artificial reef (in clean water) out of old automobile tires. Sport fishermen and scientists had long known that fish flourished around sunken ships and junked cars dumped in the ocean. Now the FLARE scientists would learn if tires could provide a suitable habitat for fish.

They found that in a few days large numbers of young fish had moved into the rubber reef, taking advantage of the thousands of hiding places provided by the

stacks of tires. Two and a half months later, another FLARE team found that many adult fish had moved into the artificial reef community. The project pointed to a solution to the problem of disposing of worn-out tires, one of the biggest disposal problems on land. Not only does it get rid of the useless tires, but it provides new environments where fish can flourish.

Off the Bahamas stands the Perry *Hydrolab,* permanently located in fifty feet of water. This four-man habitat has been used by many different groups, mostly teams of scientists. It is also available for charter by private scuba enthusiasts, such as sport fishermen and underwater photographers. *Hydrolab* was also used in making a TV film about sharks. During this session, pictures were also taken and story material gathered for a Canadian documentary film and a new *National Geographic* book about the sea. *Hydrolab's* electric power supply comes from a fuel cell, based on the fuel cells used in the *Apollo* spacecraft. Eventually, fuel cells may be developed that are powerful and efficient enough for large, deep-water habitats.

Other countries in addition to France and the United States have developed their own habitats. Japan has one that is usable down to 330 feet. Russia has a habitat named *Sadko,* built of two steel spheres, one atop the other. It has been used in the Black Sea since 1968. *Sadko* is buoyant and is tethered to the sea floor by a heavy anchor. According to reports, it is stationed at about eighty feet, and the aquanauts using it dive to about twice that depth.

West Germany, which borders on two

seas, the North Sea and the Baltic, set up a habitat in sixty feet of water off the island of Helgoland in 1969. Its first projects involved the study of fish and lobsters in the hope of raising them commercially. But there may be other missions for the German habitat. Germany is already busily extracting oil and natural gas from the floor of the North Sea. Habitat-based divers might be very useful in this line of work, conducting searches for new deposits of oil and gas, and tending the pumping machinery and pipelines when the wells are brought in. More countries will probably develop their own underwater habitats as they see how profitably other nations have utilized the resources of the sea.

In spite of the difficulties of living in an artificial environment under many feet of water, those who have done it have been enthusiastic about the experience. One member of SEALAB II expressed everyone's feelings very well when he said:

"That was the hardest I have ever worked in my life. And it is the busiest I have ever been. I would go back right now. I didn't want to come up."

The depth limits of divers are rapidly being extended. In 1968 two divers swam out of the air lock of Link's submersible *Deep Diver* 700 feet down, spending thirty minutes collecting specimens off the hard-packed, sandy bottom. In 1972, the United States Navy announced that four men had reached 1010 feet on a saturation dive off California's San Clemente Island. Such deep dives will make deeper habitats practical, and deep-ranging submersibles will be needed to deliver men and supplies.

The diver, the submersible, and the habitat are all parts of man's efforts to investigate the sea and to utilize and enjoy its secrets. Each, in its own way, has extended man's range underwater and enabled him to move about more freely in the depths. Progress in one field has led to progress in the others.

In the years ahead, it is almost inevitable that man will turn more and more to the ocean's resources as the resources of the land run out. Submersibles and habitats will make it possible for him to reach those resources—and hopefully give him the knowledge to use them wisely.

The Russian habitat Chernomor *rests on the shore of the Black Sea. Most Russian habitats have been used at relatively shallow depths.*

SOME NOTABLE SUBMERSIBLES

Submersible	Nation	Year Launched	No. Persons Can Carry	Operating Depth	Collapse Depth	Deepest Dive as of Early 1973
Aluminaut	U.S.A.	1964	2 pilots 5 observers	8,000 ft.	—	6,250 ft.
Alvin	U.S.A.	1964	1 pilot 2 observers	12,000 ft.	—	7,500 ft.
Archimède	France	1961	2 pilots 1 observer	36,000 ft.	100,000 ft.	31,600 ft.
Asherah	U.S.A.	1964	1 pilot 1 observer	600 ft.	—	600 ft.
Ben Franklin	U.S.A.	1968	2 pilots 4 observers	2,000 ft.	4,000 ft.	2,000 ft.
Perry *Cubmarine*	U.S.A.	1962	1 pilot 1 observer	300 ft.	600 ft.	300 ft.
Deep Diver	U.S.A.	1968	1 pilot 3 observers	1,335 ft.	2,000 ft.	1,500 ft.
Deep Quest	U.S.A.	1967	2 pilots 2 observers	8,000 ft.	13,000 ft.	8,350 ft.
Deepstar-2000	U.S.A.	1969	1 pilot 2 observers	2,000 ft.	4,000 ft.	2,000 ft.
Deepstar-4000	U.S.A.	1965	1 pilot 2 observers	4,000 ft.	7,600 ft.	4,100 ft.
Diving Saucer	France	1959	1 pilot 1 observer	1,350 ft.	3,300 ft.	1,350 ft.
DOWB (Deep Ocean Work Boat)	U.S.A.	1968	1 pilot 1 observer	6,500 ft.	10,000 ft.	6,500 ft.
DSRV-1	U.S.A.	1970	3 pilots 24 rescuees	5,000 ft.	7,500 ft.	3,500 ft.
Johnson-Sea-Link	U.S.A.	1971	1 pilot 4 observers	2,000 ft.	5,000 ft.	—
Kuroshio II	Japan	1960	2 pilots 2 observers	650 ft.	1,200 ft.	650 ft.
Nekton Alpha and *Beta*	U.S.A.	1968, 1970	1 pilot 1 observer	1,000 ft.	2,500 ft.	1,040 ft.
NR-1	U.S.A.	1969	5 pilots 2 observers	classified		

Submersible	Nation	Year Launched	No. Persons Can Carry	Operating Depth	Collapse Depth	Deepest Dive as of Early 1973
Perry *PC-8*	U.S.A.	1971	1 pilot 1 observer	600 ft.	1,200 ft.	600 ft.
Shinkai	Japan	1968	2 pilots 2 observers	1,960 ft.	—	1,960 ft.
Star II	U.S.A.	1966	1 pilot 1 observer	1,200 ft.	4,000 ft.	1,200 ft.
Star III	U.S.A.	1966	1 pilot 1 observer	2,000 ft.	4,000 ft.	2,000 ft.
Sea Fleas I and *II*	France	1969	1 pilot	2,000 ft.	4,000 ft.	2,000 ft.
Yomiuri	Japan	1964	2 pilots 4 observers	1,000 ft.	1,900 ft.	1,000 ft.

MAJOR EXPERIMENTS WITH HABITATS

Name of Habitat	Nation Operating	Date	Depth of Location	Breathing Mixture	Decompression Time
Conshelf I	France	1962	33 ft.	Air	—
Conshelf II	France	1963	36 ft. (2 men at 90 ft.)	Air Helium/ oxygen	2 days
Conshelf III	France	1965	328 ft.	97.5% helium 2.5% oxygen	84 hours
Man-in-Sea I (Link)	U.S.A.	1962	200 ft.	97% helium 3% oxygen	65½ hrs. (Diver needed additional decompression)
Man-in-Sea II (Link)	U.S.A.	1964	432 ft.	90.8% helium 3.6% oxygen 5.6% nitrogen	92 hrs.
Sealab I	U.S.A.	1964	193 ft.	79.5% helium 3.5% oxygen 16% nitrogen	56 hrs.
Sealab II	U.S.A.	1965	205 ft.	77-78% helium 3-5% oxygen 18% nitrogen	31-35 hrs.
Tektite I and *II*	U.S.A.	1969-1970	50 ft.	9% oxygen 91% nitrogen	21 hrs.

Glossary

ABEAM. Perpendicular horizontally to the heading of ship.

ABYSS. A deep part of the ocean.

ACOUSTIC TORPEDO. Torpedo guided by sound.

AFT. Pertaining to the stern or after part of hull.

AIDS TO NAVIGATION. Buoys, markers, lights, bells, fog horns, radio, etc.

AIR LOCK. A double door giving access to and preserving air pressure in a submarine.

ALASKA CURRENT. Current that flows northward and westward along coasts of Canada and Alaska.

AQUALUNG. Standard type of self-contained underwater breathing apparatus.

AQUANAUT. Navy term to designate "saturation divers" who spend prolonged time at depth in a habitat on the ocean floor.

ASDIC. Echo-ranging equipment; the British equivalent of America's sonar.

ASHCAN. Depth charge.

ASW. Anti-submarine warfare.

ATTITUDE. Position of a submarine in the water.

BALLAST TANKS. Tanks used to vary trim and buoyancy of a submarine.

BEACON. A navigational aid for establishing position.

BEAM. Extreme width of a ship.

BEARING. The compass direction of an object from observer.

BENDS. An illness caused by formation of gas bubbles in blood.

BERTH. Anchorage or mooring space assigned a vessel.

BLOCKADE. Naval operation barring merchant ships from entering a port or specific area.

BLOW. To exhaust water from a submarine's tank by use of compressed air.

BOW. The front end of a ship.

BQC. An underwater communications system in sea-floor habitat and each personnel transfer capsule (PTC); in this system the human voice is carried by underwater sound waves.

BREAKWATER. Structure that shelters a port or anchorage from the open sea.

BRIDGE. Submarine structure topside that contains controls and visual communication stations.

BULKHEAD. Walls or partitions within a submarine.

BULWARK. Section of a ship's side, continued above the deck as protection against heavy weather.

CABLE. A chain of metal.

CHANNEL. A main waterway.

CHART. A map on which nautical information has been marked.

CHRONOMETER. An accurate navigational clock.

CLINOMETER. Device for measuring amount of roll aboard submarine.

COMBER. A deep water wave.

CONSHELF. Continental shelf; Captain Cousteau's saturation-diving experiments.

CONTACT MINE. Explosive designed to detonate upon contact.

DDC. Deck Decompression Chamber.

DDS. Deep Diving System; an integrated surface-ship system providing all necessary equipment for a diver to descend to the ocean depths, perform a mission, and return safely to the surface.

DEAD WATER. A thin layer of fresher water over a deeper layer of more saline water.

DEEP SCATTERING LAYER. Ocean layers which scatter sound or echo sound vertically.

DENSITY LAYER. A layer of water in which density changes sufficiently to increase buoyancy of a submarine.

DEPTH CHARGE. ASW charge dropped from ships and aircraft.

DIVING BELL. A hollow inverted vessel in which men may work underwater.

DIVING PLANES (bow and stern). Control surfaces used in directing a submarine when under water.

EBB TIDE. Continuous movement of water out of a basin or river caused by a change of tide.

ECHO. An acoustic signal which has been reflected.

EMBARK. To go aboard a ship or submarine.

ENCODE. To convert plain text into unintelligible language.

ESCAPE HATCH. Submarine compartment specially fitted as an exit to be used in an emergency.

EXECUTE. To carry out a vessel's maneuver.

FAIRWAY. The channel; the navigable part of a body of water.

FATHOM. Measure of length or depth; 6 feet.

FAULT. A rock fracture, along which one side has been displaced relative to the other side.

FENDER. A device slung over ship's side to protect against bumping.

FISH. Slang for torpedo, or towed device.

FJORD. A narrow, deep, steep-walled inlet of the sea.

FLOOD TIDE. Incoming tide.

FLOTSAM. Floating wreckage or trash.

FOUL. To entangle, confuse, or obstruct.

FRACTURE ZONE. An area of breaks in underwater rocks, such as seamounts, ridges, troughs, etc.

FRESHET. An area of fresh water at the mouth of stream flowing into the sea.

FROGMEN. Underwater demolition personnel.

GALE. Strong wind varying from twenty-eight knots to fifty-five knots.

GALLEY. Kitchen.

GANGWAY. Opening in the rail giving access to the ship.

GIANT KELP. Large vinelike brown algae, attached to ocean bottom, which can grow to 150 feet.

GRAPNEL (Grappling Iron). Small, four-armed anchor used to drag for objects lost under the water.

GULF STREAM. Current originating in the Atlantic end of the Florida Straits and running northward to the Grand Banks.

GUNBOAT. Small, moderate-speed, heavily armed vessel for general patrol and escort duty.

GUNWHALE. Upper edge of a boat's side. Pronounced GUN-el.

HAND. Member of a vessel's crew.

HATCH. Access opening in deck of a ship.

HAWSER. Heavy line of wire or fiber.

HEAVE. The motion given a ship by wave action.

HEAVE TO. Cease headway and lay at rest.

HOOK. Slang for anchor.

HOOKAH. Underwater breathing apparatus with breathing gas provided from a submersible, or habitat.

HULL. The body of a vessel.

HURRICANE. Cyclonic storm with winds above sixty-five knots.

HYDROGRAPHIC OFFICE. Navy Department that produced early charts and navigational publications. Now called the United States Naval Oceanographic Office, Suitland, Maryland.

ICO. Interagency Committee on Oceanography, the top national planning council for oceanographic matters.

INCLINOMETER. Instrument for measuring the roll of a submarine.

INNER SPACE. Popular term used to designate area below surface of the sea.

JAMMING. Deliberate radio or radar interference.

JETSAM. Material which sinks when thrown overboard.

JETTISON. Throw an object over the side.

JETTY. Pier or breakwater extending into the water to protect channel or shoreline.

KEEL. Central, longitudinal beam or timber of a ship from which the frames and hull plating rise.

KNOT. Unit of speed equal to one nautical mile (6,080 feet) per hour.

LAGOON. A shallow sound, pond, or lake.

LANYARD. Small line made fast to an object to secure it.

LASH. To secure with a line or wire.

LEADLINE. Lead with attached line, used for taking soundings.

LEEWARD. Away from the wind; direction toward which waves are traveling.

LIE-TO (Lay-to). To stop a vessel without bringing it to anchor.

LOCH. An inlet or arm of the sea.

LOG. Device for measuring a ship's speed and distance.

LOSS. Large Object Salvage System.

MANEUVER. The skillful operation of a ship or submarine.

MAN-IN-THE-SEA. Programs to extend man's underwater work capability.

MINE VESSEL. Those designed to plant or sweep mines.

MINEFIELD. An area in which mines have been placed.

MINESWEEPING. Countermeasures calculated to clear a specific area of suspected mines.

MOCK-UP. Model or replica, often in life size.

MONITOR. A fighting craft used in the Civil War.

NAVAL OCEANOGRAPHIC OFFICE. The office within the navy that produces navigational charts, publications, and oceanographic information.

NAVIGATOR. Officer responsible for the safe navigation of a ship.

OCEANOGRAPHY. The study of the sea.

OFFICER OF THE DECK. An officer in charge who represents the ship's captain.

ORIENT. To find the right direction.

PATROL. Systematic and constant observation along a line to prevent the enemy from crossing it.

PERISCOPE. An optical device of mirrors and prisms, for use in a submarine.

PHANTOM BOTTOM. False bottom registered by electronic depth finders.

PICKET. Ship or submarine stationed in relation to a formation or in a geographical location.

PIER. Structure for mooring vessels.

PILING. Wood, concrete, or metal poles driven into river or sea bottom for support or protection of wharves.

PILOT. An expert on local harbor conditions.

PING. An acoustic pulse signal projected by an underwater transducer.

PITCH. Rising and falling of a ship's bow or stern in a rough sea.

PRESSURE HULL. The cylindrical, pressure-resistant core of a submarine that encloses all operating spaces.

PRIZE MONEY. In earlier times, prize money was paid a crew for the capture of an enemy ship.

PTC. Personnel Transfer Capsule, or pressurized elevator to lower and raise aquanuts.

RADAR. Radio detection and ranging, an instrument for determining, by radio echoes, the presence of objects and their range.

REACTOR. A nuclear installation releasing energy.

RED TIDE. Discoloration of surface waters caused by concentration of microscopic organisms.

RESCUE CHAMBER, SUBMARINE. Device used in removing men from a sunken submarine.

RESERVE OF BUOYANCY. Amount of buoyant volume a submarine may lose before sinking.

RIPS. Turbulent agitation of water generally caused by the interaction of currents and wind.

RUM. Remote Underwater Manipulator, a seabed recovery vehicle.

SALINITY. Quantity of dissolved salts in seawater.

SALVAGE. To save or rescue material that has been lost.

SALVAGE MONEY. Money divided among crew that has saved, or salvaged, another ship.

SATURATION DIVING. Concept in which a diver lives in a chamber on the bottom of the ocean, which is pressurized to outside water pressure.

SCREW. Propeller of a submarine or ship.

SCUBA. Self-Contained Underwater Breathing Apparatus.

SCUTTLE. To sink a submarine or ship deliberately.

SHIP MOTION. There are six different motions a submersible might develop:
  (1) Heave. An up-and-down motion.
  (2) Surge. A fore-and-aft motion.
  (3) Sway. An athwartship motion.
  (4) Roll. Heeling from side to side.
  (5) Pitch. Fore-and-aft angular rotation.
  (6) Yaw. Horizontal angular rotation.

SHOAL. An area of shallow water.

SILENT RUNNING. Condition of quiet operation of machinery in a submarine to deny detection by those listening.

SNORKEL. Device used by a submarine to enable it to draw air from the surface while submerged.

SQUALL. Short but intense windstorm.

SS. Submarine.

SSK. Antisubmarine submarine.

SUBMARINE ESCAPE LUNG. Oxygen breathing device that permits men to escape from a sunken submarine.

SUBMARINE RESCUE CHAMBER. Device lowered to a sunken submarine to be fitted over a hatch.

SUBMARINER. Man assigned to duty on a submarine. Accent on the third syllable: subma-REENer.

SURGING. Motion of a ship in which it pushes forward and aft alternately.

SWEAT. Condensation formed on inside metal surfaces of a submarine or oceanographic submersible.

TANK. Diving chamber ashore.

TENDER. Logistic support and repair ship.

TIDE. The periodic rising and falling of the earth's oceans and atmosphere, caused by the moon and sun acting on the rotation of the earth.

TIN FISH. Slang for torpedo.

TOPSIDE. Slang used by aquanauts for the surface.

TORPEDO. Self-propelled underwater explosive weapon.

TORPEDO RUN. Actual distance a torpedo travels to target.

TORPEDO TUBE. Device for launching torpedoes.

TRAWL. A funnellike net to catch bottom fish by dragging along the bottom.

TRIM TANK. Forward and after variable ballast tanks in submarine.

UNDECKED. Not having a full deck, as in case of rowboat.

UNDERTOW. A seaward flow near the bottom of a sloping beach.

UNDERWATER DEMOLITION UNIT. Team of specially trained explosive experts.

VESSEL. By United States statutes, includes every description of craft, ship, or other contrivance capable of use as a means of transportation on water.

WAKE. The region of turbulence to the rear of a submarine in motion.

WARHEAD. Forward section of a torpedo that carries explosive.

WATCH. Duty periods at sea; normally four hours long.

WATERLINE. Line of intersection of surface of water and hull of ship.

WEAVING. Zigzagging a ship.

WEIGH. To hoist the anchor.

WHARF. A mooring for ships built parallel to the waterfront.

WINDWARD. The direction from which the wind is blowing.

YAWING. A ship when rotating about her vertical axes during a heavy sea.

YAWL. Small craft having two masts, the after one being shorter.

Bibliography

Beebe, William. *Half-Mile Down*. New York: Duell, Sloan and Pearce, rev. ed. 1951.

Cable, Frank T. *The Birth and Development of the Modern Submarine*. New York: Harper & Bros., 1924.

Caidin, Martin. *Hydrospace*. New York: E. P. Dutton & Co., Inc., 1964.

Cohen, Paul. *The Realm of the Submarine*. New York: The Macmillan Company, 1969.

Colden, Cadwallader. *The Life of Robert Fulton*. Privately printed, 1817.

Cousteau, Jacques-Yves. *The Silent World*. New York: Harper & Bros., 1953.

Delaplaine, Joseph. *Delaplaine's Repository of Lives & Portraits of Distinguished American Characters*, vol. 1. Privately printed, 1815-16.

Dickinson, H. W. *Robert Fulton, Engineer and Artist*. London: John Lane, 1913.

Dugan, James. *Man Under the Sea*. New York: Harper & Bros., 1956.

Ellsberg, Edward. *Men Under the Sea*. New York: Dodd, Mead & Co., 1939, 1951.

Flexner, James. *Inventors in Action*. New York: Crowell-Collier, 1962.

Gordon, Bernard L., ed. *Man and the Sea*. New York: Natural History Press, 1970.

Guthrie, John. *Bizarre Ships of the 19th Century*. Cranbury, N.J.: Barnes, 1970.

Lake, Simon. *Submarine*. New York: D. Appleton–Century Co., 1938.

———. *The Submarine in War and Peace*. Philadelphia: J. B. Lippincott, 1918.

Latil, Pierre de. *Man and the Underwater World*. London: Jarrolds, 1956.

Marine Technology Society. *Progress into the Sea*. 1970.

Morris, Richard K. *John P. Holland, 1841-1914, Inventor of the Modern Submarine*. Annapolis: Naval Institute Press, 1966.

Piccard, Jacques, & Dietz, Robert S. *Seven Miles Down*. New York: G. P. Putnam's Sons, 1961.

———. *The Sun Beneath the Sea*. New York: Charles Scribner's Sons, 1971.

Shenton, Edward H. *Diving for Science*. New York: W. W. Norton & Co., Inc., 1972.

———. *Exploring the Ocean Depths*. New York: W. W. Norton & Co., Inc., 1968.

Singer, Charles, ed. *A History of Technology*, vols. 1-5. New York: Oxford University Press, 1956, 1958.

Sueter, Sir Murray F. *Evolution of the Submarine Boat*. Portsmouth, England: J. Griffin & Co., 1907.

Toudouze, Georges G. *Le Sous-Marin, Roi de la Mer*. Paris: Librairie A. Lemerre, 1902.

Index